To Jerry,
the first apostle I ever met.

And to Dotty,
who dared.

What Readers are Saying

Believe Like Jesus is more than just a book. It is a road map for anyone seeking to deepen their faith and actively engage with the world around them. In a time filled with uncertainty and challenges, this insightful guide encourages readers to embrace the transformative power of faith, not as passive believers but as dynamic agents of change.

Rachel Gilmore
Pastor & co-author of *Followers Under 40*

Believe Like Jesus will change the way you think about faith. More than that, Rebekah Simon-Peter's book will change the way you put faith into practice. You will want to read this book more than once to glean all the insight she shares from her years of experience.

David Livingston
Pastor & author of *Getting to Good*

Rebekah Simon-Peter's *Believe Like Jesus* is a deeply meaningful book that invites readers to move beyond simply having faith *in* Jesus to embodying the faith *of* Jesus. She challenges us to embody a more engaged and bold faith that not only knows about Jesus but also experiences the courage of Jesus personally, daring us to trust in the One whom Jesus trusted. She offers probing questions and examples of how to become more aware of the power of God in our lives. Simon-Peter powerfully weaves in her own story, along with the stories of her husband and others, sharing the challenges of life and the world and the strength of a deep and transformative faith. *Believe Like Jesus* is a must-read for anyone wanting to cultivate a faith that reflects Jesus's boldness and love and deepens their spiritual journey.

Rev. Kristopher R. Sledge
Pastor & co-author of *Followers Under 40*

A good coach motivates others to act on a new vision of what is possible. With this book, *Believe Like Jesus*, Rebekah Simon-Peter has taken this spiritual gift and put it in written form. She coaches us beyond mere discipleship and gives practical guidance to become active, called, and sent agents of God's light and love. I commend this book to all who dare to not only believe *in* Jesus but also believe *like* Jesus, to all who are inspired to live with purpose and to make a life-giving difference in the world.

Michael Roberts

Author of *Wanting More: Advent, Christmas, and Epiphany Inspired by the Teachings of John Wesley*

Today's world needs leaders willing to replace fears and doubts with spiritual and temporal power by believing like Jesus! Rebekah boldly invites us to upgrade our role as partners in Jesus's vision from disciples to apostles. She makes us believe we can shift our worldview, faith, and culture. Read this book if you want the courage to dare to *Believe Like Jesus.*

Bonnie Ives Marden

Author of *Church Finances for Missional Leaders*

We are made of heaven and we are made of earth.

The work of faith is to merge these worlds and realities,

embracing them as unified rather than hierarchical.

Arianne Braithwaite Lehn[1]

40 Days to Spiritual Transformation

BELIEVE
LIKE
JESUS

Rising from Faith *in* Jesus
to the Faith *of* Jesus

Market
Square
BOOKS

REBEKAH SIMON-PETER

BELIEVE LIKE JESUS

Rising from Faith *in* Jesus to the Faith *of* Jesus

©2024 Rebekah Simon-Peter

books@marketsquarebooks.com
141 N. Martinwood, Suite 2 • Knoxville, Tennessee 37923

ISBN: 978-1-950899-88-3

Printed and Bound in the United States of America
Cover Illustration & Book Design ©2024 Market Square Publishing, LLC

Editor: Sheri Carder Hood
Cover Design: Kevin Slimp
Page Design: Carrie Rood
Post Production Editor: Ken Rochelle

Scripture quotations used with permission from:

NRSV

New Revised Standard Version Bible, copyright © 1989 National Council
of the Churches of Christ in the United States of America.
Used by permission. All rights reserved worldwide.

ESV

Scripture quotations are from The ESV® Bible (The Holy Bible, English Standard Version®), ©
2001 by Crossway, a publishing ministry of Good News Publishers.
Used by permission. All rights reserved.

NIV

Scripture quotations marked (NIV) are taken from the Holy Bible,
New International Version®, NIV®. Copyright © 1973, 1978, 1984, 2011 by Biblica, Inc.®
Used by permission of Zondervan. All rights reserved worldwide.
www.zondervan.com The "NIV" and "New International Version" are trademarks
registered in the United States Patent and Trademark Office by Biblica, Inc.®

NLV

Scripture quotations marked NLV are taken from the New Life Version,
Copyright © 1969 and 2003. Used by permission of Barbour Publishing, Inc.,
Uhrichsville, Ohio 44683. All rights reserved.

Contents

INTRODUCTION

Toward a More Active Faith

The world is in quite a state. Wars of aggression and hatred. Terrorist attacks. Climate change. Regressive social policies. Political divisions wider than the Grand Canyon. Gun violence and mass shootings every time you turn around. The unknown impacts of artificial intelligence. Threats to democracy. A creeping sense of hopelessness.

It's tempting in these perilous times to give in to doubt, fear, and despair. To isolate, rather than to connect. To hide, rather than to shine. To shrink in our faith, rather than expand.

But we can't do that. That's not who we are. That's not what Jesus wants for us, and it's certainly not how he lived in his time on earth. Though we look to the Kingdom of Heaven for our eternal reward, we can't forget our call to create the Kingdom of Heaven on earth.

There's a saying often attributed to Mahatma Gandhi: "Be the change you wish to see in the world." This advice carries particular weight for Christians. The world can use some of that change—a lot of that change—right about now. As Christians, we've always been asked to live our faith out loud. While we may feel silenced by the sheer number of challenges

1

we face, the present times demand that we dig deep into our spiritual lives so we can be bold voices for love, for a shared purpose, and for a common vision. By living our faith in Jesus, we can transform the world and manifest the Kingdom of God here on earth.

I've prayed about this often and deeply. What does this actually mean? How can we use our faith *in* Jesus to transform the world?

The more I've thought about it—the more I've prayed about it—the more I've come to realize that faith *in* Jesus may only be a first step. When we have faith *in* Jesus, aren't we putting the load on him? Aren't we asking him to be responsible for fixing things? Aren't we letting him do most of the hard work? This kind of faith is passive. How is that being the change we wish to see in the world?

To rise to the challenge of our times, we must draw on a more active faith. We must transform our faith so that it has a greater impact. As Christians, by definition, we all have faith in Jesus. But what if we changed our mindset? What if we rise from having faith *in* Jesus to having the faith *of* Jesus?

Think about that. That's profound. That's transformative.

Faith *in* Jesus gives us someone to follow. That's not a bad thing. We all need someone to inspire the good in us—"the better angels of our nature," as Abraham Lincoln put it in his First Inaugural Address.[2] Who better than Jesus? But faith *in* Jesus puts the locus of agency outside ourselves. Like there's nothing we ourselves can do.

When we take on the faith *of* Jesus, however, we find agency resides within us, instead of outside of us. We activate and expand the faith we already have. Instead of just believing *in* Jesus, we also begin to believe *like* Jesus. As our souls are infused with Jesus' kind of faith, we become ever more Christ-like. Not only do we tap into Jesus' divinity, but we also tap into our inner divinity. And we become miracle-makers alongside Jesus.

Lest this sound heretical, let me assure you that rising from faith *in* Jesus to the faith *of* Jesus is a very biblical concept. It's the difference between being a disciple and an apostle, a distinction I'll explain in more depth in the chapters that follow. For now, think of a disciple as a follower, a student, an apprentice, and think of an apostle as an ambassador, a messenger, a journeyman or -woman empowered to act on their own on behalf of the one who sent them. The goal of embracing the faith of Jesus is to advance from being a disciple to being an apostle. In fact, that's always been the purpose of following Jesus: to be sent by him out into the world, to do the kinds of things he did.

That's the transformation of the title, a transformation that is spiritual, yes, but one that also has implications for how we live our lives. This spiritual transformation allows us to embrace our inner divinity as fuel for us to live differently. It's a two-fold undertaking: deepen your spirituality to broaden your impact. Just as a tree puts down deep roots to grow tall, we take a deep inward journey of spiritual transformation to rise into human beings who live more courageously, more miraculously. Your new way of being will invite others to do the same. As you deepen your spirituality and broaden your impact, watch the people around you become less fearful and more hopeful.

If you don't get what I mean just yet, that's okay. We have the 40 days to spiritual transformation to figure it out, a journey and practice we discuss in the rest of this book.

PART 1

The Journey Begins:
From Disciple to Apostle

Welcome to the 40 days to spiritual transformation. This is a fresh approach to spiritual growth unlike anything you may have experienced before. These 40 days of transformation invite you to shift from believing *in* Jesus to believing *like* Jesus, from rising from faith *in* Jesus to the faith *of* Jesus, from being a disciple to being an apostle, all to become more Christ-like.

CHAPTER 1

Welcome to the 40 Days
to Spiritual Transformation

I promise that this 40-day journey with Jesus will forever change the way you look at yourself, your walk with God, your faith, and your world. You will emerge prepared to live, think, pray, and act not just as a disciple but as an apostle. In fact, during this journey, you will learn the powerful differences between discipleship and apostleship.

Before now, you might not have given this distinction much thought. You might never have considered yourself a disciple, let alone an apostle. So the first thing to understand is the word "disciple." If you have desired to learn about Jesus, to emulate him in some way, or to try to follow his teachings, then you are already a disciple. Let that sink in. Discipleship is not about perfection or mastery. It's about learning and following. As I noted in the Introduction, "disciple" means student or apprentice.

Now that you realize you are already a disciple, it's time to say yes to Jesus and rise to the next level of spiritual growth by becoming an apostle. During this journey of transformation, you'll see that Jesus not only allows but encourages you to take this step of faith. You'll learn how and why to advance from one spiritual level to the next. As part of this process of spiritual evolution, or more accurately, spiritual elevation, I'll introduce you to the vital distinction between believing *in* Jesus and believing *like* Jesus, as well as the difference between having faith *in* Jesus and having the faith *of* Jesus. We'll also look at the Five A's of Apostleship—how being an Anointed, Appointed, Authorized, Accountable Ambassador of Jesus can elevate you to the next stage of Christian spirituality and enable you to tap into your inner divinity.

Why Forty Days

At this point, you might be wondering why I chose to make this a 40-day journey to spiritual transformation. What's so special about the number forty?

I mean forty days, both literally and metaphorically. Literally, you can structure this 40-day journey of transformation to take place in a season of personal spiritual growth or during a church season, such as between Ash Wednesday and Easter or between Easter and Pentecost. A practice like this is a powerful catalyst for elevating your faith and belief and transforming your spiritual consciousness and capacity.

Metaphorically, the number forty has great significance as it is used in the Bible, especially when it comes to lengths of time. But before I tell you about that, first let me say more about the significance of numbers in general.

The Significance of Numbers

Numbers have long held special meaning, culturally and personally. Many of us have our lucky numbers—I'm partial to threes and fives myself—while many cultures ascribe particular significance to specific numbers as both lucky and unlucky. In many Western countries, the number thirteen is considered unlucky, whereas in China, the number four is considered unlucky. In the West, the numbers three and seven are often considered lucky. In China and Norway, the number nine is considered lucky. I'm not even talking about the intricate calculations and interpretations of numerology—the mystical belief in the relationship between numbers and events. I'm referring to the way we think about numbers in our daily lives, especially regarding time.

This hit home with my husband, Jerry, and me when we recently had the privilege of becoming foster parents of two little brothers. When these adorable boys first came to live with us, they were four and five. It was insightful to observe how they related to time. "Five minutes" for them was both an interminable length of time and not enough time. It was interminable (and excruciating) when they had a five-minute timeout. It was never enough when they wanted to play on their iPads.

One hundred for the boys meant anything big or long. "How long until we get to go back to Sunday School?" One hundred. "How long until we get to see our Dad?" One hundred. It wasn't one hundred days or one hundred months or one hundred years. Just one hundred. One hundred represented to them the biggest span of time they could grasp.

But if they wanted to name an even longer period of time beyond their ability to grasp, they called it "post-infinity." I don't know where they first heard this concept or if they understood what it means. But it was the way they named a really long period. How long until their birthdays? Post-infinity. Sometimes, post-infinity became post-infinity plus one hundred! That was a really, really, really long time—how long it was until Christmas, for example. While these numbers didn't make logical sense to the rest of us, they had internal coherence for the boys.

Lengths of Time in the Bible

In the Jewish Torah and the Christian Bible, as well as in other sacred writings, numbers have long held spiritual value and internal coherence. Even so, the biblical writers didn't adhere to strict time frames. They didn't have appointment books, digital calendars, or clocks synced to Greenwich Mean Time. They lived within the cycles of nature. They marked time by sunrise and sunset, the number of stars visible in the sky, the phases of the moon, agricultural seasons, and the length of the reign of a king (and every once in a while, a queen).

These are very practical uses of time. Some spans of time are more symbolic. In particular, three such spans are often repeated in the Bible: three days, seven days, and forty days. Twelve is another number with biblical significance. Twelve refers to the number of sons of Jacob, who became the heads of the twelve tribes of Israel. In an intentional parallelism, the first group of disciples, also known as apostles, were said to have been twelve in number, too.

According to the *Dictionary of Biblical Imagery*,[3] three days means a few days. Jonah is in the belly of the whale for three days just as Jesus is in the tomb for three days. The three-day periods don't mean exactly seventy-two hours as we would think today. It simply means more than one day. These aren't exact chronological measurements.

Seven days means a complete set of days. For instance, the fullness of creation consists of seven days: the first six days of creation plus the day God rests. We also see that meaning reflected in the use of the number seven, such as in the seven

churches of Revelation, the Seven Deadly Sins, named by
Pope Gregory I in the sixth century, and the Seven Heavenly
Virtues. In Matthew (18:21), Jesus uses multiples of seven to
describe the number of times we are called to forgive others:
seventy times seven.

The Power of Forty Days

When it comes to lengths of time, forty days has particular
significance. Forty days means a relatively long time, long
enough to serve as a period of transformation. For instance,
Noah's flood lasts forty days—enough time for humankind
to undergo both correction and redemption by God. Jesus'
spiritual forebears, Moses and Elijah, both fast for forty days
and forty nights. During that time, Moses meets God on Mount
Sinai. Elijah, for his part, hears the still, small voice of God.
After their ordeals, they emerge with new insight and a deeper
connection with God. These times of fasting and contemplation
bring about spiritual transformation. In the same way, Jesus
fasts for forty days and forty nights, during which he is
tempted by Satan and redeemed by God. In these forty days,
Jesus undergoes a spiritual transformation in preparation for
his three-year public ministry.

Thus, symbolically, forty days represents spiritual
transformation, a transformation that generates a change in
identity, a maturation, an elevation, a new way of being in the
world where the individual acknowledges and accepts their
higher purpose.

That's why I chose forty days for the spiritual practice set
out in this book. I invite you to join me for a 40-day period of
spiritual transformation, of advancing from discipleship to
apostleship. Keep in mind that, just as forty days represents

a symbolic period of time in the Bible, so it does in this book. You won't need to complete the practice in exactly forty days (unless you want to). Take what time you need to participate in the spiritual awakening and growth that God opens up for you. The insights you receive, the new vistas that open for you, the revelations you encounter, and this transformation take place uniquely between you and God. As the biblical writers came to understand, never underestimate the power of spending prolonged time in the company of God and the presence of the Holy Spirit. Who knows, your journey might even take you post-infinity plus one hundred! The point is to give yourself to this journey of transformation, no matter how long it takes. Like Noah, Moses, Elijah, Jesus, and countless others who have given themselves to an intentional period of spiritual formation, you will be amazed at the spiritual insight and divine connection that emerges within you.

For that reason, I have created "A 40-Day Guide to Spiritual Transformation" for you to consult, found in Appendix A at the back of this book. This 40-day guide will walk you through a series of reflections drawn from the book's contents to facilitate your spiritual transformation.

Sharing This Journey with Others

You can embark solo on this journey of spiritual transformation, or you can do it with others in community. Moses, Elijah, and Jesus journey solo. Yet, the disciples who follow Jesus experience transformation in community. While no one disciple has the same journey, the Gospels are clear that the disciples follow Jesus as a group, a band of committed friends. So it is in the presence of Jesus and each other that the disciples' journeys of transformation to apostles takes place.

In the same way, you may have a group of family, friends, or fellow spiritual seekers with whom you would like to share this path. Invite them to join you for the journey of a lifetime!

The Goal: Spiritual Elevation to Co-Create Miracles with God

In this 40-day journey to spiritual transformation, you'll be challenged to master new mindsets and expand your beliefs. Out of these new beliefs, you will learn to take new actions. As you take new actions, you will see yourself and others in new ways. These new perspectives will reveal new ways of being. As you believe, act, and perceive in expanded ways, the world around you will shift, too. Your shift in consciousness and capacity will prompt a shift in the people and culture around you. Ultimately, you will be the change you wish to see in the world.

Both John the Baptist and Jesus himself demonstrate this truth. They each undergo a period of contemplation and transformation to grow in the knowledge and grace of God before they begin their public, prophetic work. Their inner work is a prerequisite to co-creating miracles with God. You are being called to do the same thing—to transform the nature of your spirituality from believing *in* Jesus to believing *like* Jesus, from having faith *in* Jesus to having the faith *of* Jesus, all so you can advance from discipleship to apostleship and live out your miraculous new life.

CHAPTER 2

Do You Have the Faith of a Mailman?

"Do you think I'm an apostle?"

It was an unusual come-on from a would-be suitor. As a single female pastor, though, I had gotten used to fielding all kinds of odd subjects on first dates. One guy only wanted to discuss Bible studies. Talk about not being able to leave my work at the office! Another guy wanted pastoral counseling about getting back together with his former girlfriend. I'm not sure he understood the irony of that request. A third guy wanted to get my take on why bad things happen to good people. I would have to pull out my old theology books for that one.

But this was a first. Did I think this guy was an apostle? My first thought was, does he have delusions of grandeur? On the next date—if there was going to be a next date—would he ask me if I thought he was Napoleon?

No, his question seemed sincere. I learned that five years earlier, he had hit rock bottom—drugs, alcohol, the works. But now he was living clean and sober and experiencing a close relationship with Jesus for the first time in years. His whole life was turning around. I could see the fire in his eyes and hear the passion in his voice. The truth is, we met in recovery. A few years earlier, I, too, had cleaned up my act after years of using drugs and alcohol to solve problems they were never

15

meant to solve. That's when I received the call from Jesus to be a pastor. I guess my date that night figured it would be safe to ask me his question.

Honestly, I wasn't sure how to answer. I was a fairly new Christian myself. Not only that, but this man was a Catholic, and I didn't think Catholics talked about apostles; it seemed like more of a Pentecostal thing. And he was a mailman. It was the first time I had heard someone outside the ministry even mention the word "apostle," let alone apply it to themselves. "Apostle" seems reserved for the select few or as a synonym for "disciple." Or maybe, as I thought at the time, for Pentecostal leaders. But mail carriers? I wasn't sure.

"Do I think you're an apostle?" I echoed, stalling for time.

"Yeah," he said. "Do you think I'm called to bring people to Jesus?"

I paused. I really wasn't sure if bringing people to Jesus made him an apostle. I simply hadn't given the notion much thought.

I fell back on the age-old trick of stumped teachers and workshop facilitators everywhere. "Let me get back to you on that."

That simple question sent me on a years-long journey that has led me to this book. Was this man an apostle? For that matter, am I an apostle? What exactly is an apostle anyway?

The Secret Faith of Apostles

I discovered one thing right away in my research. "Apostle" is not an exact synonym for "disciple." Some faith traditions blend the two words and blur the distinction between them. I can see why this blending and blurring

16

happens. In the Bible, the same set of people are sometimes called disciples and sometimes apostles. However, the problem with blending and blurring the two terms is that it calls us to do and be more without equipping us with the faith to do so. This book aims to give you not only a picture of the differences but the theological underpinnings necessary to *Believe Like Jesus*. So let's take a closer look at the origin and meaning of the two words, disciple and apostle.

The word "disciple" comes from the Latin *discipulus*, meaning student or pupil. The word "apostle," on the other hand, comes from the Greek *apostolos*, meaning envoy. As you can see, not only do the two words come from different languages, but they also have distinct connotations.

A disciple is the student of a particular teacher. A disciple's primary focus is the teacher and mastering their teachings so they can follow the teacher's path.

In the New Testament, we learn that the Pharisees, John the Baptist, and Jesus all have disciples. In those days, it was common for these kinds of teachers to have students. Of all three, we know the most about Jesus' disciples. In fact, much of the Gospels is devoted to stories about the disciples' adventures with Jesus. These disciples travel extensively with Jesus to learn all they can about his life and ethos. That means they learn from Jesus while together on the road, while resting, at mealtimes, and in fellowship with friends. They follow his path. In fact, when Jesus says in John 14:6 (NIV),[4] "I am the way and the truth and the life," he recalls the Hebrew word *derech*, which means road, path, or way.

Although the list of disciples' names that Jesus calls varies depending on the Gospel, the number is always the same: twelve. Sometimes, they are even simply called "the Twelve."

Regardless of the particular names, twelve people functioned as disciples learning from Jesus, the rabbi, the teacher. But that wasn't all Jesus had in mind for the Twelve. He wanted them to become apostles as well.

While a disciple is a student, an apostle is an altogether different animal. The word "apostle" means envoy, one sent forth. If disciples are followers of a teacher, apostles are agents of that teacher. Seen this way, disciples are somewhat passive, while apostles are active, even proactive. Apostles are messengers sent out as commissioned agents to act on behalf of another person, in this case, Jesus. Apostles represent Jesus in the world. They are acting for Jesus. They are acting like Jesus.

In fact, we can see that Jesus means for the Twelve to represent him right from the beginning. Check out this passage from the Gospel according to Mark 3:13-15 (ESV):

> *And he went up on the mountain and called to him those whom he desired, and they came to him. And he appointed twelve (whom he also named apostles) so that they might be with him and he might send them out to preach and have authority to cast out demons.*

From the beginning, Jesus is clear about his larger purpose. He calls the Twelve to be his students so that after teaching them what they need to know, he can send them out as his agents and envoys. Jesus doesn't simply teach them about the kinds of things he does. Jesus teaches them how to *do* what he does: preach, heal the sick, and cast out demons. He isn't offering them knowledge to pass some final exam. This is practical knowledge they will use to pray and act in his name when he sends them out as his emissaries to the world. In fact, every time we pray and act "in Jesus' name," we are declaring our own apostleship.

To be Jesus' emissaries, the Twelve must take on spiritual authority and technical know-how. This is why Jesus teaches them to go beyond simply having faith *in* him to embracing the same kind of faith he has. Otherwise, they could never do the things he does.

These Twelve are followed by the Seventy-Two (or Seventy in some translations) and later by those who hadn't traveled with Jesus during his lifetime, including Paul, Silas, Barnabas, and Junia. These four apostles emerge after Jesus' public ministry, death, and resurrection.

Jesus doesn't call the Twelve or the Seventy-Two or any of the others to be mere followers. Yes, they are there to learn from him. However, being a follower is simply the first stage in their spiritual development. It's not the end. Apostleship is the ultimate goal of their training. Jesus invites them to follow so that when the time comes, he can send them into the world to take his place as agents of spiritual transformation in the lives of others.

During the three years the Twelve spend with Jesus, they observe how he thinks and prays. They watch how he teaches and note the way he deals with naysayers. They watch him engage paralyzed, hurting, and desperate people. They listen to how he speaks, what he speaks about, and the way he communicates with all kinds of people. The Twelve are even privy to his miracles. But the learning doesn't stop there. Because Jesus aims to transfer his spiritual authority, agency, and accountability to them, the Twelve also observe his inner relationship with God and soak up what he believes. They must do so if they are to speak, act, and heal on behalf of him and the Kingdom of God and be active agents and stewards of the Kingdom dream. I wrote about this extensively in my book

Dream Like Jesus: Deepen Your Faith and Bring the Impossible to Life.[5] What is Jesus' big dream? "Thy kingdom come, thy will be done, on earth as it is in heaven" (Matthew 6:10 KJV).

Who gets to be an apostle today? Sometimes, we think apostleship is reserved for those who launch churches or go on mission trips to faraway countries. I disagree. In fact, after my date with the mailman, I began to look at apostleship in a whole new way. I realized apostleship doesn't have to be your full-time job. It is more of an approach to your relationship with Jesus. By studying Jesus' model of spiritual growth, I see that apostleship is the natural next step after discipleship. In Greek, as noted earlier, "apostle" refers to one who is sent out as an envoy or emissary, a representative, on behalf of the teacher. If the Twelve had only functioned as disciples by following Jesus, his message would have died when Jesus died. But because the Twelve go out as apostles, they are able to spread the teachings of Jesus. In fact, their willingness to be apostles is why we know about Jesus and call ourselves Christians today. In the world of social media, it's the difference between having likes and followers on your Facebook or Instagram page and having influencers who promote you and direct people to your site.

At a deeper level, though, the difference between disciples and apostles is not so much what they do as much as what they believe. Or, to flip it around, once they transform what they believe about themselves and their relationship with God, true apostles do what follows naturally.

Disciples and apostles have qualitatively different kinds of faith. Disciples have faith *in* Jesus, while apostles have the faith *of* Jesus. They don't only believe *in* Jesus, but they also believe *like* Jesus. Otherwise, there's no way the Twelve or Seventy-Two could ultimately do what Jesus does. Even while

Jesus is alive, they heal the sick, cast out demons, and preach the Kingdom. They have authority over unclean spirits. After Jesus ascends into heaven, their power continues and expands. In fact, the book of Acts is known as the Acts of the Apostles because most of it takes place after Jesus' death, resurrection, and ascension. Acts details the life of the early church and the spread of Christianity made possible by these disciples-turned-apostles. Acts is filled with stories of the miracles they perform. Acts 5:12 clearly states: "The apostles performed many signs and wonders among the people."

The more the apostles heal people, the more others are drawn to learn about Jesus. As their belief in Jesus grows, they, too, bring the sick and suffering into the streets to be healed. This, in turn, empowers the apostles even more. Peter's very shadow seems to bring healing, as shown in Acts 5:15: "As a result, people brought the sick into the streets and laid them on beds and mats so that at least Peter's shadow might fall on some of them as he passed by." As author Bonnie Ives Marden noted to me, "This is biblical evidence of miracles accomplished by disciples who transform into apostles through their belief and actions. How easily we step over this evidence!"

Rising from Faith *in* Jesus to the Faith *of* Jesus

What does that really mean when we say disciples have faith *in* Jesus, but apostles have the faith *of* Jesus?

Faith *in* Jesus means trusting in his power, his love, his teachings, and his saving grace. This is the kind of faith you learn about in church—in Sunday School messages to children and youth groups, as well as in songs and hymns, sermons, and Bible studies. Faith *in* Jesus is the focus of much teaching on salvation. How do you get saved? You must believe in Jesus, and then Jesus will save you. There's a kind of passivity to that relationship. If I hold certain beliefs, something good will happen to me. I will be saved. "I will be saved" is grammatically in the passive voice. Where's the agency in that?

I know I'm exaggerating here. There's a lot of good to be said about believing in Jesus. Personally, it has made a big difference in my life. It has helped me grow in calm and confidence, knowing that Jesus is there for me. I'm not knocking it. What I'm trying to put forth is that this kind of belief is a first step—an important first step—but only a first step in the Christian journey. Just as Jesus wasn't a passive person, we friends of Jesus aren't called to be passive either. As recipients of Jesus' love, teaching, and healing, we are called to be proactive. We dare to build on our faith *in* Jesus to rise into the faith *of* Jesus.

Having the faith *of* Jesus takes faith to a whole new level. It means trusting in what Jesus trusts in. Having the faith *of* Jesus means abiding in a deep knowing that you are one with God and one with the Holy Spirit. It means living in constant communion with and surrendering to God. It means living with an ever-ready expectancy of miracles. It means cultivating unwavering trust in your life purpose. It means entertaining a rock-solid knowledge that all things are possible, even resurrection.

In other words, having the faith *of* Jesus means operating in an elevated state of consciousness in which there is no separation between humanity and divinity, between us and God. When we take on the faith *of* Jesus, we become more like Jesus. Even though this notion is a big part of the New Testament, it's not emphasized in church services or Bible studies. Yet the Gospel according to John especially focuses on the deep unity we share with Jesus. "I am the vine; you are the branches. If you remain in me and I in you, you will bear much fruit; apart from me you can do nothing" (John 15:5). We are invited to sense this deep unity with the divine within ourselves.

It can be scary or disorienting to think of faith in this way. You may say, "Look, Rebekah, I'm a disciple. I can't be an apostle. I'm not good enough. I'm nothing special. I don't even go to church." Or "My church doesn't talk about disciples. It never mentions apostles. I wouldn't even know where to start." Or even, "I know me. No way am I one with God."

I get it. However, I challenge you to rethink that notion. If you pay attention to the stories of the Twelve in the New Testament, you'll see that the end game is always apostleship. If we are invited to see ourselves in the Biblical stories, then, just as the Twelve are called, you are called. Just as the Twelve are anointed, you are anointed. Just as the Twelve are appointed, you are appointed. Just as the Twelve are authorized, you are authorized. Just as the Twelve are accountable, you are accountable. Just as the Twelve are ambassadors of the Kingdom, you are ambassadors of the Kingdom. These are the Five A's of Apostleship, which we will discuss at greater length in Chapter 10.

The point is, just as Jesus calls to him those whom he desires so he can send them out to do the work of the Kingdom, Jesus calls you. You see, I believe that discipleship was always and only meant to be the first step in your relationship with Jesus. Rising into apostleship is how Jesus' ministry is carried out. Even when you shrink away from seeing yourself as a carrier of divine gifts, Jesus remains openhanded, reminding you that the gifts are yours to claim. The invitation to apostleship is yours to accept.

Apostolic faith is powerful. Get ready for a shift. Once you step into it, your consciousness and capacities expand. As a disciple, you may feel like there's not much you can accomplish, influence, or change in this world. But apostolic faith moves mountains and mulberry trees. In the Gospel according to Matthew, Jesus answers his disciples' question about why they can't cast out a demon that was besieging a boy. "He said to them, 'Because of your little faith. For truly I say to you, if you have faith like a grain of mustard seed, you will say to this mountain, "Move from here to there,"' and it will move; and nothing will be impossible for you'" (Matthew 17:20 ESV). This is a huge promise. Taken at face value, it's overwhelming. You might be tempted to write it off. But this isn't an isolated teaching.

There's a similar exchange in the Gospel according to Luke. In this passage, Jesus is teaching about the necessity of forgiving again and again. "The apostles said to the Lord, 'Increase our faith!' And the Lord said, 'If you had faith like a grain of mustard seed, you could say to this mulberry tree, "Be uprooted and planted in the sea," and it would obey you'" (Luke 17:5-6 ESV).

Even though the passages reflect different aspects of Jesus' teachings, Jesus' response is surprisingly similar. Both passages compare faith to a grain of mustard seed.

I used to think that Jesus was saying the apostles' faith was too small. After all, Jesus calls the Twelve's faith "little" in Matthew. I thought Jesus was saying that their faith was even smaller than a grain of mustard seed. Have you ever seen mustard seeds for sale in the grocery store or online? They're pretty small. If you're not reading closely, you can think that Jesus is commenting about the size of the apostles' faith. Pay attention to the next part of the sentence, however:

"If you had faith like a grain of mustard seed, you could say to this mulberry tree, 'Be uprooted and planted in the sea,' and it would obey you'" (Luke 17:6). In Matthew 17:20, Jesus refers to moving a mountain, not a mulberry tree. Both tasks feel like impossible tasks. How could a small grain of faith accomplish either one?

But, contrary to some interpretations, I don't think Jesus means to say that even the smallest faith, if genuine, can move something as rooted as a tree or a mountain. No, it isn't about the size of their faith. Instead, I think Jesus is referring to the hardiness of this tiny seed, and, by extension, the hardiness of the disciples' faith.

As a one-time Master Gardener in Wyoming, I know this about seeds: they are hardy. They need to be to penetrate tough soil as well as to survive the shivering spring, the heat of summer, the frost of fall, and the frozen winter. Tiny little seeds like mustard push aside roots and rocks, other plants, and even concrete to grow.

Given the nature of seeds, I think Jesus is talking about the persistence of the mustard seed, not its size. It's a fair comparison. So often, we give up on our faith. We self-sabotage by not following through on our beliefs. We give up on ourselves, and we give up on God. We lower our expectations about what is possible. But, mustard seeds don't do that. They grow everywhere. And they grow into large plants. They don't stunt their own growth or doubt their capacity to become what they are created to be. Here's the first lesson in apostleship: Don't give up on yourself, and don't give up on your faith. Jesus calls us to single-minded growth and purpose in our faith, undivided by doubt, unbowed by pressure, and undiminished by circumstance. I believe Jesus

25

is saying that if you have faith that doesn't give up on itself, nothing can stand in your way, not even things that seem immovable. Not mulberry trees, not mountains, not anything. This persistent faith in God and in oneself is the kind of faith Jesus encourages us to pray for. It's the kind of faith the apostles pray for when they say, "Lord, increase our faith" (Luke 17:5 ESV).

I call this request, "Lord, increase our faith," the prayer of the apostles. It's a deceptively simple prayer. Yet, it's the kind of prayer that empowers us to advance from discipleship to apostleship. As an aspiring apostle, I invite you to make this prayer your prayer, too. Before you pray it, though, let's consider the word "faith." The online *Oxford Dictionary* defines "faith" as "complete trust or confidence in someone or something" or "Strong belief in God or in the doctrines of a religion, based on spiritual apprehension rather than proof." Often, people turn to Hebrews 11:1 (ESV) for a biblical definition of faith: "Now faith is the assurance of things hoped for, the conviction of things not seen."

Each of the definitions has something in common. They imply that deep levels of trust are required for faith, even in the absence of evidence.

When we talk about faith and what it means, it's important to pay attention not only to the word "faith" but also to the subject of that faith. In the New Testament, a tiny Greek word makes a world of difference. Often translated as "in," the word can also be translated as "of." So, rather than faith *in* Jesus, the phrase could be rendered as the faith *of* Jesus. According to certain scholars, "Many newer translations of the Bible render certain verses written by the Apostle Paul to say that we are to live by our faith IN Christ—

whereas the earlier King James Version translated these to say that we must have the faith OF Christ."[6]

It's interesting that the earlier King James translation of verses, such as Galatians 2:16, Philippians 3:9, and Revelation 14:12, in which the phrase "faith of Christ" appears rather than the phrase "faith in Christ," are now being reclaimed as more accurate. This is more evidence for advancing from discipleship to apostleship.

My faith *in* Jesus rests on the trust that Jesus is there for me. That he won't leave me or abandon me. That I have a relationship with Jesus, who is out there, separate from me. That by my faith, I trust him to make good things happen for me by virtue of his divinity. That through my belief in him, he will guide me as a mentor and as a teacher. I ask for help, knowledge, and wisdom, and through my faith *in* Jesus, Jesus provides these. It's almost like a child-parent relationship wherein I am protected. I love this sense of protection. But at some point, even children must leave home. When they don't, we call it failure to launch.

As we "adult" and venture out on our own, we aim to embody whatever positive traits our parents or guardians have taught us. We go out into the world to make our own way. Likewise, having the faith *of* Jesus means I am ready to "adult" in my spiritual life and take greater responsibility for my faith. That in my imperfect human way, I am ready to become more Christ-like. That I will not merely trail behind Jesus, but be sent to represent him. This brings us back to believing *like* Jesus believes, believing the same way Jesus believes, not just believing in Jesus. I like that scholars have arrived at this conclusion, too. It is interesting how changing one little preposition from "in" to "of" expands the scope of faith in a major way.

With all this in mind, here we are. You are invited to take the next natural step in your spiritual journey with Jesus by praying the prayer of the apostles. To not only believe *in* Jesus but also to increase your faith to believe *like* Jesus. To refrain from self-sabotage by not giving up on yourself or God. To not only have faith *in* Jesus but to have the faith *of* Jesus.

Before we pray the prayer of the apostles, first notice one more thing: this prayer is written in the plural, "Lord, increase *our* faith." As you dare to pray this prayer, know that you are not alone. With this prayer, you are joining a global community of people taking this transformational step of faith, as well as the great throng of witnesses who have come before you, steeped in this faith. Feel them with you and around you as you open your heart and mind in prayer.

Ready? I invite you now to pause and pray with intentionality the prayer of the apostles: "Lord, increase our faith." And like the faith that is as a grain of mustard seed— hardy, persistent, capable of growth—let that faith grow from within you. Amen.

Did you do it? Don't skip this important step.

Alright, now that you have prayed, "Lord, increase our faith," let the prayer resound within you. Let it become part of your very cells. And let it become the foundation of your daily prayer life. At the same time, don't confuse the prayer of the apostles with the Apostles' Creed. The Apostles' Creed is a post-biblical summary of the Christian faith, developed in the fourth century, for people getting baptized. It contains the basic teachings for someone taking the first steps into discipleship. The prayer of the apostles is biblical, and is designed for those taking the next step beyond discipleship. It's the prayer that Jesus himself directs the apostles to pray. And it's yours to pray again and again. After all, if a small-town mail carrier can envision himself as an apostle, why not you?

Back to that date over twenty-four years ago. After the mailman asked me whether he was an apostle, I had to question my own level of faith. After all, he was a mailman, and I was a pastor. Where in the heck was my trust in God? Maybe this guy was an apostle. After all, as a mailman, he had been delivering messages for years. I prayed my own version of the prayer of the apostles when this same mailman eventually asked me another big question. This time on bended knee. Eight months later, we married; we have been persisting like the grain of mustard seed since then, expanding in love and faith for the last twenty-three years.

I can report that my husband, Jerry, while no longer a mailman, is most definitely an apostle—a messenger of light, of hope, and of recovery. He hasn't started churches or baptized anyone, but he has brought many to belief in God by showing others how to live free of drugs and alcohol, as himself has done for decades. For almost thirty years, he has mentored and encouraged dozens and dozens of people seeking to live life clean and sober by finding a higher power to guide them in their recovery.

Putting the Prayer of the Apostles into Practice

As you pray the prayer of the apostles found in Luke 17:5, "Lord, increase our faith," begin to feel the expansion of faith within you. Notice how your doubt shrinks as you pray, how your resilience grows, and how your persistence increases. You are becoming a miracle-maker, the kind of person who can move mountains and cast mulberry trees into the sea. So keep praying the prayer of the apostles.

Now that you have opened your heart and mind to pray the prayer of the apostles, it's time to explore what it means to transform your faith. It's not just more of the same kind of faith of believing *in* Jesus. Instead, we will explore what it means to have the faith *of* Jesus and believe *like* Jesus.

PART 2

Your 40-Day Journey:

Believe *Like* Jesus

To transform your faith to the faith *of* Jesus over these forty days, you are invited to learn what Jesus believed and, more importantly, how to believe *like* Jesus. This is how you can shift your consciousness, transform your spiritual beliefs, and rise from discipleship to apostleship. Remember that you can also consult Appendix A to follow along with "A 40-Day Guide to Spiritual Transformation."

CHAPTER 3

The Five Beliefs of Jesus Will Transform Your Life

If we are going to talk about believing *like* Jesus, we have to know what we mean by the word "belief." What is a belief? How do we come to believe? Can we change our beliefs?

A belief is a practiced way of thinking, of accepting that something is true, sometimes without physical evidence or logical proof. Research shows there are three kinds of belief: facts, preferences, and ideologies.[7,8] For instance, "Grass is green" is a fact-based belief. "Fries are better than onion rings" is a preference-based belief. "There is only one true way to God" is an ideological belief.

When we dig a little deeper, ideological beliefs actually contain a mixture of facts and preferences. For example, the existence of about thirty-three thousand different Christian denominations suggests that even people who hold some common beliefs have preferences mixed in, preferences that are strong enough to launch whole new denominations.

Consider how different Christian denominations handle baptism. Methodists and Catholics both baptize babies, although for different reasons. Baptists, however, wait until a child is old enough to choose baptism for themselves. Or what about the matter of when and how to serve Holy Communion? Should you use wine? Is grape juice acceptable? Do we drink out of a common cup? Or does everyone get their own cup? Or should we dip into a common cup instead of drink out of it? Should Holy Communion be offered every day, once a month, or once a year? Do the elements of communion literally turn into the body and blood of Christ, as Catholics believe, or is this a symbolic remembrance of Jesus' last supper, as Protestants believe? There are even different beliefs about Jesus. Some Christians focus more on his humanity and others on his divinity. Some focus more on his crucifixion, others on his resurrection. Some believe he is an exemplar for how we are to live. Others believe there's no way we can even begin to live like he did.

Studies show that by age five, children hold all three kinds of belief—fact, preference, and ideological—and that many of the beliefs we hold for a lifetime get formed at this early age. As a result, it often takes great effort to shift beliefs, our own and those of others.

For instance, as children, we may believe we need our special blanket to be safe in the world. We may believe that one kind of cereal is preferable to another. We may believe that a younger sibling is horning in on our parents' attention. For a while, our foster kids believed there was no way they could fall asleep in our home without two stories and two songs. No matter how tired they were, they wouldn't close their eyes until both stories had been read and both songs had been sung ("Lullaby and Good Night" and "You Are My Sunshine," were the songs in case you were wondering).

Sometimes, beliefs are based on fairy tales and superstitions. As a child, I believed in the Tooth Fairy, Santa Claus, and the Easter Bunny. I believed a Magic 8 Ball could tell the future. I believed if I stepped on a crack, I would break my mother's back (well, not really, but it was a game we played).

Over time, as I grew older and developed the capacity to reason, logic began to inform my beliefs. I left fairy-tale beliefs behind and embraced new ones. I believed if I worked hard and listened to my teachers, I would always do well. I believed if I was a good person, kind and loving, only good things would happen to me. Later, I believed drinking and drugging made me cool. That belief didn't work out so well and thankfully I let it go.

But there are other beliefs I have hung on to that don't necessarily serve me. I have discovered that sometimes working hard is not enough. Bad things do happen to good people who are kind and loving, and there's no use pretending otherwise.

Even as you mature and shift from one belief to the next, you, too, have probably hung on to beliefs that don't serve you. We don't automatically outgrow all the beliefs that no longer fit. Instead, we live with many of them unconsciously, and they influence our decisions and the way we think about the world. If you grew up in a household where affection was withheld, for example, you might believe the world is a harsh and heartless place and that you don't deserve to be loved (even by God), even if you know better intellectually. To break these negative thought patterns, we must periodically examine our beliefs with intention and release those that no longer serve us. For instance, if we persist in believing we are unlovable, then love may perpetually elude us.

This 40-day journey to spiritual transformation invites you to become more conscious of what you believe so you can release limiting beliefs and consider new beliefs that will further your journey of spiritual growth.

Beliefs are extremely powerful and stubborn, however.

We don't easily give them up. Try telling a three-year-old
that the Tooth Fairy or Santa Claus isn't real. Try explaining
to a straight-A student why they didn't get the scholarship
they applied for. And we all know that friend or relative who
believes with all their heart that the world and everyone
in it is out to get them. They feel cheated by life and make
themselves—and others around them—miserable because of it.

Beliefs have power, whether for good or for ill. In Mark
6:5-6, the gospel writer notes that in his own hometown, Jesus
"could not do any miracles there, except lay his hands on a
few sick people and heal them. He was amazed at their lack of
faith." Somehow, without the faith of the townspeople, Jesus'
own power for healing isn't enough to effect change.

The good news is that if a lack of belief can keep you from
healing, the opposite is also true. As Jesus notes many times,
your faith can make you well, both spiritually and physically.
Remember the story of the woman who had been bleeding
profusely for twelve years? Mark 5:25-34 relates her story. This
determined woman had tried everything over the years—
doctors, cures, remedies—but nothing had yet staunched the
flow of blood. When she has the chance, this woman slips into
the crowds around Jesus, saying to herself over and over, "If
I touch even his garments, I will be made well." She pushes
through, reaches out, and touches his cloak. Immediately, she
felt within herself that the longtime bleeding had stopped. At
the same time, Jesus realizes that "power had gone out from
him," even as the crowds push him forward. That's when he
looks around for who has touched him. Realizing Jesus is
looking for her, the woman catches up with him and tells him
what happened. Jesus says, "Daughter, your faith has made
you well; go in peace, and be healed of your disease."

The healing power of faith isn't just biblical metaphor. Modern science agrees with Jesus. In his book *The Biology of Belief,* the cellular biologist and lecturer Bruce Lipton presents evidence that what you believe goes a long way toward keeping your body healthy—that your thoughts and beliefs can change things at the cellular, even genetic, level. Without going too deeply into the science, Lipton's big insight is that genes don't control the cell—that genes don't predetermine an outcome—but rather, the cell's environment, including our thoughts and beliefs, controls the expression of the DNA in the body. While today, this field of study is known as epigenetics, in Jesus' day, this would have been called healing.[9] While not all scientists agree with Lipton, Lipton demonstrates the possibility that our beliefs are critically important to our physical, mental, and spiritual health.

The most important of our beliefs concerns our relationship with God. Many of us have been taught to believe that we are separate from God and that we must spend a certain amount of energy or intentionality getting and keeping God in our lives—that God is somewhere out there, and we have to work hard to find God or find someone who can take us to God. We probably don't even know how we acquired this belief. But it's a dangerous one. If we can be separated from God, then we have no anchor, hope, or real grounding in this life.

No matter how we have acquired such beliefs about God or ourselves, these beliefs shape our experience of life. Our beliefs shape what we expect, what we experience, and what we imagine is even possible. For example, if you have ever prayed for and received a miracle of healing, as did the woman who was bleeding for twelve years, then you know the miraculous power of belief *in* Jesus. Now Jesus invites you to take it one step further by adopting the same kind of faith he has.

If we have the faith *of* Jesus, if we believe *like* Jesus, we can co-create miracles with God and influence the very nature of our experience of life. We don't even have to look outside ourselves to do so. As we step into the spiritual power God has intended for us all along, we advance from being a disciple to being an apostle.

Believe *Like* Jesus and Shift Your Consciousness

Some people don't believe they could ever be apostles and are content to remain disciples. (For that matter, others don't believe they can even be disciples. They are content to be observers.) But if we have learned anything from the stories of the disciples in the New Testament, it's that discipleship and apostleship are deeply connected. The Gospel of Mark makes this relationship plain. Right from the beginning of the Gospel, in Mark 1:17, Jesus links following him with being sent out by him. "Come follow me," he says to two brothers, Simon and Andrew, who are fishing on the lake, "and I will send you out to fish for people." Mark 3:14-15 reinforces the connection between following and sending: "He appointed twelve that they might be with him and that he might send them out to preach and to have authority to drive out demons."

Advancing from discipleship to apostleship was the natural progression for the the Twelve and the Seventy-Two, and it is for us as well.

How do you undertake this journey of a lifetime? Prepare to embrace five beliefs of Jesus that are reinforced throughout the Gospels. As we discuss each one, I'll set out specific steps you can take to believe *like* Jesus and put your spiritual transformation into practice. I'll also share how I am taking these steps myself.

What Jesus Believes

1. **Partnership with God:** Jesus believes that he and the Father are one. He understands at a deep level that there is no separation between him and God and between him and the Holy Spirit. Through this divine partnership, Jesus not only has peace but is encouraged, emboldened, and empowered. It's the consciousness in which miracles can occur.

2. **Prayer has Power:** Jesus believes that his prayers have power. Jesus speaks often in the Gospels about how he believes God hears and answers his prayers and how his prayers have life-changing positive effects on others. Indeed, through these prayers, Jesus demonstrates his unity with God and performs miracles.

3. **Miracle Mindset:** Jesus believes the miraculous is possible because he is one with God and his prayers have power. Jesus cultivates this miracle mindset that allows the impossible to become possible. Not just once in a while, either. But all of the time. Because of Jesus' miracle mindset, he is known for his ability to heal almost everywhere he goes.

4. **Life has Purpose:** Jesus believes his life has a compelling purpose, and his larger purpose is to bring the Kingdom of Heaven to earth. This purpose guides him in his daily life and ministry. His miracles are a sign of the presence of the Kingdom of Heaven on earth.

5. **Resurrection is Real:** Jesus believes that resurrection is real. Although his friends don't understand it, Jesus senses all along that crucifixion won't be the end of him. He knows he will rise again. Resurrection is the ultimate miracle. It is available for all of us.

Expanding from faith *in* Jesus to the faith *of* Jesus, from disciple to apostle, is not as much about what you do as what you believe. Think of each of these beliefs as a transforming principle that will take you deeper into your soul, higher into consciousness. They even enable you to experience your inner divinity. Tapping into your inner divinity like this will, in turn, fuel your rise from disciple to apostle. Consult "5 Steps to Co-Creating Miracles with God," in Appendix B at the back of the book, for a creative process that turns the mundane into the miraculous, using the five beliefs of Jesus.

Then let's take a closer look at each of the five beliefs of Jesus, starting with a partnership with God.

CHAPTER 4

Believe in Your Divine Partnership

Jesus believes that he operates in divine partnership with God. This relationship is especially apparent in the Gospel according to John, the most supernatural of all four Gospels. John begins with the words, "In the Beginning was the Word and the Word was with God, and the Word was God" (John 1:1).

Let me say more about "the Word," which here refers to Jesus. In early Christian theology, the Greek philosophical term *Logos* signified the divine wisdom and order in the cosmos. It's translated as "word," "reason," or "plan." So, when we talk about *Logos* in a Christian context, we're referring to the divine reason that gives everything order, structure, and meaning.

Of all the Gospels, John uniquely identifies Jesus Christ as the incarnate *Logos*, or "Word." This concept is critical for understanding why Jesus believes in partnership with God. The use of the term *Logos* tells us that Jesus existed before his earthly life and was with God from the beginning. As the *Logos*, Jesus is the agent of creation and the one who reveals God's plan of salvation to us. As the *Logos*, Jesus is the bridge between God and the world, helping us understand God and God's will.

Elsewhere in John, Jesus sums it up this way: "I and the Father are one" (John 10:30). This powerful statement from

Jesus directly ties into the concept of *Logos* in several ways. First, it speaks to Jesus' unity with God. Jesus' claim that he and the Father are one affirms his divine nature as the *Logos*. As the *Logos*, Jesus doesn't just bring a message from God. Rather, Jesus is the living embodiment of God's wisdom and plan. Second, Jesus believes his unity with God should be apparent through his many good works. You can hear this in the following passage:

> *Jesus declares, "Anyone who has seen me has seen the Father." Then he asks Thomas and Philip, "How can you say, 'Show us the Father'? Don't you believe that I am in the Father, and that the Father is in me? The words I say to you I do not speak on my own authority. Rather, it is the Father, living in me, who is doing the work."*
>
> **John 14:9-10**

Humanity and Divinity are Inseparable

When Jesus says he believes he is one with God, he means there is no separation between them. As the Gospel of John puts it in John 14:11, "I am in the Father and the Father is in me."

You might say, "Rebekah, of course God and Jesus are one. He is the Christ, the Son of God." The Gospel of John reinforces this high view. But we also have to remember that Jesus is fully human, too. When born into this world, he is subject to all the uncertainties of human life, with its trials and tribulations. In his humanity, I believe Jesus shows us how to embrace our inner divinity and our oneness with God. The Gospel of John also points to this. Jesus says, "On that day you will realize that I am in my Father, and you are in me, and I am in you" (John 14:20). Not only are Jesus and God one, but we are part of that divinity, too. Put another way, divinity is within us, somehow expressed through our humanity.

What does it mean for you and me to be one with God? Your first thought might be that being one with God means being pure and without sin. Think about that, though. If we have to be without sin to be one with God, then unity with God is impossible and the scriptures are wrong. But unity, by definition, takes us beyond dualistic thinking into a new realm of experience.

Consider the words of 20th century Christian mystic, Thomas Merton, whose personal experience gives us a glimpse into this unity.

> *The fact is... that if you descend into the depths of your own spirit... and arrive near the center of what you are, you are confronted with the inescapable truth that, at the very root of your existence, you are in constant and immediate and inescapable contact with the Infinite Power of God.*[10]

Is this the divine unity that Jesus experiences with God?

If at the very root of our existence lies the Infinite Power of God, then like Jesus, like Merton, we too are invited to acknowledge and experience this divine unity, this oneness with God. In fact, we exist within it, and it exists within us.

In the week before the crucifixion, Jesus deepens the concept of unity and explicitly includes the disciples.

> *I will remain in the world no longer, but they are still in the world, and I am coming to you. Holy Father, protect them by the power of your name, the name you gave me, so that they may be one as we are one.*

John 17:11

43

I have given them the glory that you gave me, that they may be one as we are one— I in them and you in me— so that they may be brought to complete unity. Then the world will know that you sent me and have loved them even as you have loved me.

John 17:22-23

Here, "they" and "them" are the disciples, of course, those whom Jesus has taught throughout his ministry, his followers. Now, Jesus is pointing to something more, a greater role for them. Although the Gospel of John never uses the term "apostle," you can see that Jesus is promoting his disciples to apostles in the sense we have defined: the emissaries he's leaving behind in the world to take on his work. To do so, they need to take on the faith *of* Jesus, "that they [the apostles] may be one as we [Jesus and God the Father] are one." To be an apostle rather than a disciple, to have the faith *of* Jesus rather than merely faith *in* Jesus, each of the Twelve must be one with God as Jesus is one with God. And they must be one with each other, expressing the divine unity within them.

Jesus manifests his belief in divine partnership in his words—in this case, his prayer to his Father—and in his works. Not too long after this prayer comes the Passion, where Jesus gives himself up to be crucified and, ultimately, to be resurrected. As you develop the faith *of* Jesus and believe *like* him, you'll see that, like Jesus, both your words and works are imbued with divine unity.

Becoming One with God

Embracing new beliefs requires a dedication to spiritual practice. Practice, in this sense, doesn't mean "rehearsal," as in doing a dry run of a stage play, gymnastics routine, or speech.

Its meaning is more like "discipline" in the sense of mastery, for example, of yoga, meditation, or playing a musical instrument.

For each of the beliefs of Jesus we discuss in this chapter and the next four, I set out spiritual practices to help you transform your beliefs and to help you believe *like* Jesus. Think of these practices as only a beginning. An important leg of the journey from disciple to apostle is figuring out what works best for you.

Here are two spiritual practices—one based on words and the other on works—that will help you rise from disciple to apostle.

Words: Say It and Make It So

Throughout history and all the world's myths and literature, words and naming have always held great power. In Genesis, God speaks the entire world into existence, beginning with bringing order out of chaos and then light out of darkness. The Word is not only creative but also divine. Each day of creation brings new life until the world is teeming with the beauty of nature and humanity. The Gospel of John echoes Genesis. As you and I are made in the image and likeness of God, we, too, have this inborn capacity to speak things into being through the creative power of the spoken word. Just as "Logos" is the divine word, so when I declare, "I am one with God," I take a sacred first step toward acknowledging my own unity with God.

How does this work in practice? First, put yourself into the scripture as Jesus did: "I and the Father are one." As I repeat these words and meditate on them, I am filled with a deeper sense of God's presence in me. I have found that I can amplify this feeling by also addressing myself in the second person:

45

"Rebekah, you and the Father are one." Or even in the third person: "Rebekah and the Father are one."

Talking to yourself in the second or third person has surprising effects. Scientists have found that talking to yourself in this way helps with emotional regulation and distance. In other words, it gets you out of your head and helps you become more objective about your condition or state of mind. If you're trying to change the way you think about something, for example, if you want to change your belief about how you and God are one, addressing yourself in the third person detaches you from your ego, from your investment in the way things are, in how you don't want things to change. It's always easier to give someone else advice, right? This is a form of that.[11]

You may feel some doubt as you speak these words to yourself, whether in the first, second, or third person. Notice where the doubt is located in your body. Is it in your head or in your heart? Your head—headquarters of ego, fear, and self-doubt—may want to talk yourself out of believing you are one with God. If so, turn to your heart—your local hub for God-consciousness and divine connection. Notice how your heart responds as you repeat these words. You may sense both hesitation and transcendence. That's likely how the disciples feel, too, as they begin to believe *like* Jesus. At the same time, feeling those feelings frees you up to tap into the divine power within you to do what's required of an apostle.

Works: Do It and Make It So

Through your faith *in* Jesus, you likely have already done many good works. You have undoubtedly tried to emulate the love and kindness of Jesus. You have demonstrated kindness and compassion toward others. You have helped people in need. You have prayed for the sick and suffering. You have lived out your faith *in* Jesus.

Now, as you rise from having faith *in* Jesus to developing the faith *of* Jesus, I invite you to change how you may think of these good works. Instead of thinking of your good works as leading you to God or things you do for God, try thinking of it this way. Consider that your good works arise from your oneness with God and express your partnership with the divine.

Here's how to make that shift. Consider the good works you have already done. Think about who you have prayed for, cared for, blessed, and given to. Include the projects you have undertaken, the leadership you have offered, and the behind-the-scenes know-how you have given. Make a list of these good works. Then, celebrate them. I mean really celebrate them! Not for ego fulfillment but as a way of acknowledging your very real partnership with God. Doing these good works could not have happened without a holy collaboration between you and God. Both your contributions and God's contributions are essential. In fact, it is God working through you that even allowed these good works to happen.

As you strengthen the belief that you are one with God, this belief will not only change the way you look at yourself, but it will also change your perceptions and the way you live your life.

Embrace the Changing Belief: You Are in Partnership with God

As you work through this spiritual practice, you will notice that a new space opens up within your belief system to embrace the belief in your partnership with God. Even so, your old beliefs may get in the way, and your negative self-talk may persist. Change is hard. You may find yourself bumping up against what seems like an impossibility. Your ego is attached to the way things are. "What will it mean to see myself as one with God?" "How will it change my life?" "My life isn't so bad right now ..." Change is hard and scary. You may be tempted to cling to the status quo.

How do we overcome this resistance? By learning to embrace the belief that we are one with God on a deeper level, the level of our soul.

The ancients long believed that to be human is to house the divine within the body in the form of a soul. More recent spiritual teachers have a different take on it. In a quotation attributed to Pierre Teilhard de Chardin, a Jesuit priest and paleontologist, by way of self-help author Wayne Dyer and business author Stephen Covey, "We are not human beings having a spiritual experience. We are spiritual beings having a human experience."[12]

Think about that! What a transformative way to look at ourselves. This perspective gives primacy to our divine natures. It turns on its head what we are doing here—on earth, in this world, in this body, in this life. By putting our divine selves front and center, we foreground our partnership with God. This frees us to release the (very real) human doubts and negativities that hold us back. This frees us to believe *like* Jesus and embrace the faith *of* Jesus.

Recently, I attended an international conference where I met delegates from around the world to share my work. I felt intimidated—overwhelmed and disconnected from my spiritual power. I wasn't sure that little old me, all five-three-and-one-quarter of me, could rise to the occasion. When I meditated in my downtime, a new image came to me. I saw my soul envelop my body. It was a warm, vibrant green that surrounded and embraced me. That changed my perspective. I envisioned my soul lifting me up and carrying me along. After that, I could meet each day with confidence, connecting soul to soul with each person I met. I truly felt the Christ in me was meeting the Christ in each of them. Perhaps this idea of the soul surrounding the body is what the ancient art of iconography was trying to represent by including halos and discs of light around the heads of holy people in statues and paintings.

The scripture is clear. Whether the soul houses the body or the body houses the soul, we are not complete beings without the Spirit of God. Take, for instance, Ezekiel's vision of the valley of dry bones coming back to life in Ezekiel 37:4-6 (ESV). Listen as God directs Ezekiel to speak to the dead bones:

> Prophesy over these bones, and say to them, 'O dry bones, hear the word of the Lord. Thus says the Lord God to these bones: Behold, I will cause breath to enter you, and you shall live. And I will lay sinews upon you, and will cause flesh to come upon you, and cover you with skin, and put breath in you, and you shall live, and you shall know that I am the Lord.'

Ezekiel does as directed. Then God shows Ezekiel how the bones are now covered with sinew, flesh, and skin. But it isn't until God causes the breath to enter them that the bones truly come alive. In both Hebrew and Greek—the languages of the Bible—the word translated as breath also means spirit and wind. Breath is holy, divine, and spiritual. Our bodies are sustained by the Spirit and presence of God.

But unity with God is bigger than what happens within

your body or your soul—as if either could be disconnected
from the larger whole. As I wrote in *Dream Like Jesus*:

> ... *if God is everywhere present, not a discrete being in the
> sky, but the quality of Being itself, that means that each of
> you is inside of God, and God is inside of each of you. You are
> surrounded by, and suffused with, Divine Power. You live
> in a deeply interrelated ecosystem of the Divine, of Life, of I
> Am-ness, where everything is interconnected and interrelated.
> By virtue of your inclusion in the creation, you are already one
> with Jesus and with God. It's how things are made.*[13]

When you believe *like* Jesus does—that you are in true
partnership with God—you act with the understanding that God
is always present in you and works through you in all you do.

What Would an Apostle Do?

As you grow in belief in your partnership with the divine,
pay attention to new actions the Spirit is prompting you to
take. When you believe that God is with you always, that you
are with God always, and that even if you don't feel it, you and
God are inseparable, the impossible starts to seem possible.
Especially when you preference the encouragements of your
heart over the cautions of your head. For instance, what evil
or injustice can you now address? What kindness or healing
can you now offer? What words of love or acts of hospitality
can you now risk? What interest or gift within you can you
now cultivate and share?

Jesus teaches the apostles how to do the things he did
and how to tap into the miraculous to do so. The apostles
cast out demons, heal the sick, and proclaim the Kingdom.
Clearly, they have to believe as Jesus does to accomplish these
astounding deeds.

As I take the 40-day journey with you, I, too, am tapping into my partnership with God. It's a big order, so I'm starting small. Instead of self-sabotaging, I am learning to be self-supporting. Why? Because to self-sabotage is to say that I don't deserve to experience unity with God, or I don't deserve to feel the flow of divine power with me, or heck, I don't even deserve to feel the flow of self-support. One of the many ways I have self-sabotaged is by denying myself the very things I say I want, things that are good for me, things that are well within my reach—like getting enough sleep, drinking enough water, eating well, and having more downtime to recharge my batteries. Being self-supporting is not selfish. Rather, it's an important quality for an apostle. If we do not participate in building our own faith, we are treading water in the status quo.

It is time to step up and out of the status quo to a new level of faith. I decided to take on a new practice: the spiritual discipline of stretching my body. Stretching may not seem like much of a spiritual discipline, but consider the many ways we use the word. We say we are stretching ourselves when we grapple with new ideas, take on new actions, and try new behaviors. We say others are stretching us when they push us outside our comfort zones. We say that God is stretching us when God asks us to do different or difficult things, things we may never have thought to try, or things we know we should do but would rather not. Stretching leads to growing and evolving—to spiritual transformation.

At the same time, studies show that stretching our bodies improves mobility, mood, focus, and clarity. Stretching makes us more emotionally resilient and more self-reflective.[14,15] It's all interconnected! Since our bodies and souls are connected, I believe stretching provides even new ways of experiencing

God. I find that the more I stretch my body, the easier it is to open my heart, mind, and spirit to new ideas and new promptings of the Holy Spirit.

The Bible talks about the stiff-necked and the hard-hearted. Neither one is a compliment. The stiff-necked and hard-hearted are people who are set in their ways. They aren't open to seeing in new ways and trying new ways of thinking. They are living small. Unable or unwilling to expand their thinking or enlarge their spirit, they are disobedient—or at least indifferent—to God. While they may say they believe *in* Jesus, I doubt they would be open to believing *like* Jesus.

Something very interesting has happened as I have reincorporated daily stretching into my life. Not only has my stiff neck loosened and my flexibility returned, but the hard-heartedness that crept into my life softened and expanded, too. I have begun to yearn for music, theater, and art deeply. While I've enjoyed these to an extent in the past, I can't say I yearned for them. Out of this new yearning, I have attended a high school musical, the local symphony, a best-selling author's reading of his new book, an art exhibit of local artists, a hands-on art demonstration, and two museum installations. I even undertook my own creative project with a friend. All within a few months. Believing in my divine partnership with God, the ultimate and original creator, has reinvented me from the inside out. This is a journey of transformation I didn't see coming.

I'd love to tell you that I can suddenly draw, paint, dance, and sing like a pro. Nope. But as I have loosened up, I have developed a new appreciation of the creativity around me. At the same time, I have grown more connected to my community and made new friends. These friends have deepened my sense of belonging and brought solace into my life when my beloved mom recently passed away. Receiving the compassion of my new friends has allowed me to offer deeper compassion to those around me. All because I trusted the divine unity within me and dared to stretch in new directions.

I wonder what else believing *like* Jesus will produce in your life and mine. Dare to stretch yourself literally and figuratively. Dare to put your emerging belief of divine partnership into action by following these spiritual practices and creating your own as we journey together during this 40 days to spiritual transformation.

Belief in Action

Beliefs shape your thoughts; thoughts fuel your actions; actions demonstrate your faith, and your faith reinforces your beliefs. So, as you begin to believe *like* Jesus, you will find that you are now able to think new thoughts, take new actions, and develop new faith. Mountains and mulberry trees start to move. The people around you begin to respond in new ways. And the world becomes a brighter place.

- **Believe:** Just as Jesus is in divine partnership with God, so are you. Jesus has faith that, at a deep level, there is no separation between him and God or between him and the Spirit. That they are divine collaborators. You, too, are invited into this unity, and are an expression of this oneness. Believe it. Embrace it. Don't shy away from it. You are one with God.

- **Answer the Call:** Jesus shows his partnership with God in his words and works. Use your creative, inborn capacity to create with words—to remind yourself of your unity with God. "I am one with God." Saying the words names your belief and puts it out into the world. Contemplate your oneness with God to bring it to life. Express that divine partnership in what you do as well—in your good works. What becomes possible when you stretch and say "yes" to the needs around you? When you answer the call to help, your partnership with God will carry you.

• **Practice:** Look for opportunities to partner with God. Nina Lesowitz and Mary Beth Sammons wrote a book about courage called *What Would You Do if You Knew You Could Not Fail?: How to Transform Fear Into Courage.*[16] Let's rephrase that and ask: What would you do if you knew God was your partner? Claim the courage to see the world through that lens. Put that partnership into practice with everything you do. You and God can accomplish anything together, including miracles!

The next transformative belief of Jesus builds on partnership with God. Turn the page when you are ready to continue your 40-day journey of spiritual transformation.

CHAPTER 5

Believe Your Prayers Have Power

During this 40 days to spiritual transformation, we are learning how to expand our faith from the faith of a disciple to the faith of an apostle. That means up-leveling your faith from believing *in* Jesus to believing *like* Jesus. As you practice believing *like* Jesus, you can begin to do the kinds of things Jesus did.

In the previous chapter, we looked at Jesus' belief in divine partnership and how we can lean into that partnership to do good in the world and bring the Kingdom of Heaven to earth. The key to a good partnership is communication. That's true whether we're talking marriage, friendship, parenting, or work relationships. And it's also true in our connection with God. What form does communication with the divine take? Prayer, of course. Jesus believes his prayers have power, and he shows this time and again during his ministry.

Prayer Has Power

Jesus believes his prayers have power. In fact, he knows it. He regularly sought guidance and strength in good times and hard times through prayer.

You'd think that Jesus, being fully human and fully divine,

in full partnership with God, wouldn't need to pray. But it's this very partnership with God that makes Jesus' prayer so effective. In fact, the scriptures are full of Jesus' prayers and his talking with God. He prays throughout his life. From the moment of his baptism (Luke 3:21) to the moment of his death (Luke 23:46), Jesus prays. In between, he often withdraws from the crowds that follow him to connect one-on-one with God: "Yet the news about him spread all the more so that crowds of people came to hear him and to be healed of their sicknesses. But Jesus often withdrew to lonely places and prayed" (Luke 5:16). Here, the word lonely means quiet, uncrowded.

Jesus uses prayer for both meditation and renewal, connection and communion with God. After healing people all evening in Mark 1:35, Jesus needs to get away for some self-care: "Very early in the morning, while it was still dark, Jesus got up, left the house and went off to a solitary place, where he prayed." He does the same in Matthew 14:23: "After he had dismissed them, he went up on a mountainside by himself to pray."

Jesus also prays for the strength and power of God to work through him, for example, when he prays before choosing the Twelve: "One of those days Jesus went out to a mountainside to pray, and spent the night praying to God. When morning came, he called his disciples to him and chose twelve of them, whom he also designated apostles" (Luke 6:12-13). Even more important, Jesus prays at the Transfiguration when he reveals to the Twelve his divine nature: "About eight days after Jesus said this, he took Peter, John and James with him and went up onto a mountain to pray. As he was praying, the appearance of his face changed, and his clothes became as bright as a flash of lightning" (Luke 9:29). I can imagine Jesus asking his Father, "Is it time yet? Should we show them?" before he reveals his divine nature to them.

You get the idea. Prayer is important and essential to Jesus. He turns to prayer to center himself and renew his strength. He prays before major events in the Gospels. He prays to draw on his Father's strength. He prays even before he teaches others to pray! "One day Jesus was praying in a certain place. When he finished, one of his disciples said to him, 'Lord, teach us to pray, just as John taught his disciples'" (Luke 11:1).

Some of Jesus' most moving prayers come in the time leading up to and during the crucifixion. These prayers are sprinkled through all four Gospels. As noted in the previous chapter, Jesus prayed for himself, his disciples, and all believers right before his crucifixion (John 17). The Gospels of Matthew, Mark, and Luke all report that Jesus prays repeatedly in the Garden of Gethsemane (or the Mount of Olives) for God to redirect his path so he doesn't have to face crucifixion. Even so, each time, he also surrenders his will to God's will (Matthew 26:36-46; Mark 14:32-42; Luke 22:39-44). On the cross, Jesus even prays for forgiveness for those who are crucifying him: "Jesus said, 'Father, forgive them, for they do not know what they are doing'" (Luke 23:34). Then he prays for God not to abandon him: "My God, my God, why have you forsaken me?" (Matthew 27:46, Mark 15:34). Finally, he prays while committing his spirit to God, as he breathes his last: "When he had received the drink, Jesus said, 'It is finished.' With that, he bowed his head and gave up his spirit" (John 19:30).

Jesus believes in communication, in prayer. His prayers express his deep partnership and unity with God, whom he called Father.

Your Prayers Have Power

Not only does Jesus believe that his prayers have power, but he also believes that your prayers have power. Listen to this audacious advice from Jesus in Mark 11:24: "Whatever you ask in prayer, believe that you have received it, and it will be yours."

Whatever?! Yes, that's what the scriptures say.

"I tell you the truth," Jesus says elsewhere in the Gospels, "if you have faith and do not doubt, not only can you do what was done to the fig tree, but also you can say to this mountain, 'Go throw yourself into the sea,' and it will be done. If you believe, you will receive whatever you ask for in prayer" (Matthew 21:21-22). Does this sound familiar? It should! This promise echoes what we've already heard Jesus say to the Twelve about their faith in Chapter 2: "[F]or truly, I say to you, if you have faith like a grain of mustard seed, you will say to this mountain, 'Move from here to there,' and it will move, and nothing will be impossible for you" (Matthew 17:20 ESV).

Did you catch that? When you believe *like* Jesus, you can ask for whatever you want in prayer. All it takes is faith and belief.

And persistence.

We talked about faith, like the grain of a mustard seed, which is about persistence in faith. Jesus also teaches persistence in prayer: "Then Jesus told his disciples a parable to show them that they should always pray and not give up" (Luke 18:1). In the parable, a woman goes up against an unjust judge, seeking a fair hearing for her case. He doesn't care about others or put much stock in God. She is persistent. Still, he denies her. Yet, time after time, she persists. Finally, the judge hears her out simply because of her persistence. Jesus makes the point that if an unjust judge finally delivers justice, how much more will a just and loving God answer your prayers?

Faith, belief, and persistence are key ingredients to bring to prayer. Yet, one more quality is needed as well. This quality may surprise you: intentionality. You must intentionally allow good things to happen to you and through you. Prayer is hindered when we pray against our deepest beliefs. Rather, we need to pray in alignment with our beliefs, that is, truly believing in the power of prayer. In John 16:23b-24, Jesus says, "Very truly I tell you, my Father will give you whatever you ask in my name. Until now you have not asked for anything in my name. Ask and you will receive, and your joy will be complete." Remember we have said that praying in Jesus' name is an expression of apostleship. It's a way of affirming that we are tapping into the power of Jesus' beliefs.

You might say, "Okay, great, I want a million dollars, so let me just pray for it." But if, deep down inside, you really don't believe you deserve a million dollars, much less that you will actually receive it, then this prayer won't likely be answered in the affirmative even if you pray in Jesus' name because your beliefs aren't aligned with your prayer.

Remember, Jesus says you not only have to pray but believe that you have received what you asked for. So, I suggest you start by praying for something you can truly believe in— or at least pray for something you don't actively disbelieve or doubt you can receive. When doubt enters in, it can derail even the most beautiful prayer.

Allow Your Prayers to be Answered

Jesus assures us that our prayers are heard and answered, especially when we persist in prayer. Next, we have to allow the answered prayer to reach us.

This is how I visualize prayer working: I envision a constant conveyor belt of blessing and abundance that flows from God to us. You ask; God answers. In fact, the moment you ask for something, the answer to your prayer gets plopped on the divine conveyor belt of blessing and begins to make its way to you.

But what if, along the way, you second-guess your request? Or worry about your ability to handle the blessing? Let's say you're not sure you can integrate the new state of affairs that the answered prayer would bring into your life. Then what?

If these doubts are strong enough, I imagine they can slow down, stop, or even reverse the conveyor belt of blessings that prayer bestows. In other words, you can unintentionally work at cross purposes with your own prayers. This derails receiving your answer to prayer.

To allow God's answer to make its way to you, weed out the doubt that may disallow and derail them. Begin to notice and name the nagging doubts that accompany your prayers. As you name these doubts, return them to God on a different conveyor belt. Then ask God to strengthen your faith and increase your belief as you refocus on joyfully receiving whatever you have asked for in prayer.

I don't know about you, but I have prayed many, many prayers that never seemed to get answered. So how do I square that with the scriptures? In retrospect, I can see that no sooner had many of these prayers left my mouth than I followed them up with doubts and disbelief. It takes focus and clarity to keep a clear prayer request before God. Thus, the need for persistence in both faith and prayer.

Mindless, time-wasting activities like video games and social media (let alone physical addictions) can also block our prayers. I'm not saying we don't all need a break occasionally, but let's be honest. When what we do for a "break" becomes an obsession that takes longer than we can afford, the break becomes a blockage. That's true whether it's endless scrolling on social media sites or getting caught up in seemingly harmless video games. Personally, I've had to limit both. Otherwise, I've used my time to numb out with adrenaline and dopamine hits, rather than opening my heart and spirit to God.

We all have to open ourselves to allow God to answer our prayers.

I learned I needed to actively cultivate a new belief in my capacity to grow and the confidence that I could handle God's answered prayers. Otherwise, I would have quietly counteracted my own prayers with self-sabotage, without even knowing it. What attitudes, beliefs, fears, behaviors, or activities would you have to surrender so Jesus could answer your prayers and so you could see and hear God answer your prayers? It may not be a long list, but it's bound to be a potent one. These are the self-limiting thought patterns that may have hindered you for years.

As you release these self-limiting patterns, ask yourself what attitudes, beliefs, affirmations, behaviors, and practices you would have to adopt so God can answer your prayers.

To believe *like* Jesus, it's time to surrender the first set and adopt the second. Jesus lived in partnership with God and believed his prayers had power. To not only believe your prayers have power but to actively allow them to be answered, you'll need to revisit these commitments again and again. Apostleship is not for the faint of heart. Studies show that the brain is hard-wired for survival, for caution. But your soul is hardwired for union with God, for greatness, and for co-creating miracles with God. Let your soul lead the way in communicating with God and watch your prayers take on new meaning and power.

Rejoice and be glad! You've begun to look at faith in a

new way, the way in which apostles consider faith. You've prayed the prayer of the apostles. You've begun to expand your consciousness and capacity to grow into a new kind of Christian. You're rising from faith *in* Jesus to the faith *of* Jesus. You're advancing from disciple to apostle.

Embrace the Belief: Start Small

Several years ago, drawing upon the scripture, "Whatever you ask in prayer, believe that you have received it, and it will be yours," I put into practice the belief that my prayers had power. I asked God for something small and inconsequential that wouldn't trip the wires of self-doubt. I figured a mug would do. After all, mugs are everywhere. It wouldn't require superhuman effort to pray for the gift of a mug and believe in the power of that prayer.

I practiced believing that I had received the mug by visualizing the act of opening my hands and seeing a mug placed in them. I rehearsed the feeling of happiness that would accompany it. I did that for about a week, then I forgot about it.

One afternoon, three or four weeks later, the doorbell rang. I opened the front door of our house to a man I didn't recognize. Beyond him, I could see a weathered pickup truck parked across the street.

"Can I help you?" I asked.

"I'm Willie," he answered. "This mug is for you." He handed over a misshapen blue coffee mug, obviously handmade. "Well, for your husband, actually. I really enjoyed working for him. I made it for him after our last construction job. It's been sitting on the floor of my pickup truck for months." He nodded toward the truck behind him. "I just never got around to stopping by."

"Why, thank you," I beamed, suddenly remembering my prayer for the mug. "You wouldn't believe it, but this is just what I've been praying for."

My prayer had been answered. Like Jesus, I began to believe that my prayers truly did have power.

What about prayers for something bigger than a mug? Prayers that sincerely matter, prayers that can be life-changing?

When Jerry and I married twenty-three years ago, we wanted to have kids. But having kids naturally on our own didn't seem to work. We investigated foster parenting and took some of the training. But that didn't seem right for us at the time. Then we looked into adoption, both domestic and international. We filled out the paperwork at every stage. I regularly prayed, counting on my partnership with God to bring the right child (or children) into our lives. But somehow, none of these options seemed right either. So we didn't pursue them to the end. Finally, I prayed and, only a little facetiously, asked, "God, can't the stork just ring the doorbell and drop off a child on the front steps?" That didn't happen either. Parenthood didn't seem to be in the cards for us. I grieved and let it go. Or so I thought.

Fast-forward twenty-three years. On January 1, I faced an existential crisis, wondering if my life was worth living. Yes, I was surrounded by loving people, engaging work, and the beauty of nature. But somehow, I felt it wasn't enough. My parents were aging. Jerry and I were getting close to retirement. Several chapters of our lives would soon close, and it seemed as if nothing was waiting to replace them. While some of my friends and relatives talked about visiting their adult children and others spoke of visiting their grandchildren, taking them to the park, and attending baptisms and birthdays, all I saw ahead of me was lonely, empty time. I grew up in a large extended family on both sides. But now, all I felt was absence—the absence of my own adult children and, with it, the possibility of grandchildren. The absence of a loving family of many generations gathered together in love. The long-ago grief for not having children returned with a vengeance.

I found myself sad and crying. I was dull and listless. I didn't eat. I didn't smile. I'm sure Jerry was worried about me.

Ten days into the existential crisis, a man Jerry had been mentoring called and told him his family was falling apart. His wife was using drugs, and their two young children were in danger from the mother's neglect. The man could do little about it because he was four states away on a job site he couldn't leave. As I went to bed that night, I prayed for the family.

The next morning, I woke up and got ready for my work as a coach and consultant to church leaders. As I dressed, I realized I needed to cut a tag from a new piece of clothing. I stepped into the guest bedroom and turned on the light to look for a pair of scissors. Poking out from the white bedcovers and nestled in the pillows, I saw two heads of tousled brown hair.

"That can't be right," I thought. "Nobody's in that bed." At the same time, I flicked off the light, thinking, paradoxically, that I'd better not wake them. "Wait a second," I said, doing a double-take. I turned the light back on and looked closer. Sure enough, two little boys were fast asleep in the guest bed.

I returned to our bedroom and whispered urgently to my still half-asleep husband, "Jerry, what's going on?"

Jerry roused himself and, despite his drowsiness, knew exactly what I meant. "They'll be here for a few days until my friend can get home from the job site. I hope that's all right."

My surprise turned to wonder, then recognition and acceptance. I knew in my heart and soul that this was God's work. Here were two angels entering our lives, just not the kind with wings. God had answered my prayers—this time with more than a coffee mug.

A few days turned into a few months. We were appointed legal foster parents for the two boys, aged four and five (soon to be six). Jerry and I quickly stepped into the roles we seemed destined to play all our lives: Mom and Dad. We talked the boys through what must have been a confusing experience for them. We kept them fed, clothed, and bathed. We got them to daycare and kindergarten on time and picked them up. We made school lunches and cooked endless pots of mac and cheese. We provided them with things to do in their free time—toys and games, both electronic and real-world, visits to the local park, and arts and crafts projects.

It was all so new for us, tiring and energizing at the same time. What had we done all day before we had these two active little boys in our lives? They truly were a gift from God. I no longer had the time or inclination to dwell on my troubles. The existential crisis receded. My heart and soul soared with the grace God had bestowed on me—on us. I got to be the mom I had always wanted to be, an experience I feared had passed me by long before. I had the joy of watching Jerry be a dad, a really good dad.

Happily, Jerry and I are still involved in the lives of these boys. They stay with us whenever their father has a two-week shift at work. It turns out that parenting two weeks at a time is just perfect for us.

God answered my stork prayer after all, just twenty-three years later than I expected it, a reminder that, although God answers our prayers as Jesus promises, God does it in God's own time and way.

Which brings us right back to faith. We must embrace the faith *of* Jesus to be ready and able to recognize when our prayers are answered and act on them.

What about Heartfelt Prayers that Haven't Been Answered?

That scripture verse, "If you believe, you will receive whatever you ask for in prayer," is provocative. Like me, I'm sure you have had heartfelt prayers that haven't been answered. You have believed with all your heart and still not received what you asked in prayer. Does this mean that you derailed your own prayer with doubt and disallowing? Does this mean that Jesus isn't reliable? Does this mean that God has said no?

I remember the time when I was a pastor and led the congregation in weeks of deep, heartfelt prayer for a ten-year-old boy with cancer whose grandmother was a member of the church. Although our prayers were deep and heartfelt, the young boy died.

We weren't wrong to pray. Nor were we wrong to believe. But our prayers were only part of the equation. This little boy had his part to play as well. After all, it was his life and soul we were praying for. It turned out that he had a different prayer. Before he passed, the boy had told his grandma that he was tired and all he wanted was to be with God.

God answered a prayer all right, just not the congregation's. That's when we must trust that God knows what God's doing. That's when we have to remember our faith.

What about major systems of injustice like racism or sexism? Does the fact that they still exist mean we haven't believed hard enough or that God has said no to our prayers?

As with just about all human endeavors, it's more complex than that.

I think about how the Montgomery bus boycotts started with one woman, Rosa Parks, who bravely refused to give up her seat in the front of the bus. She and others had trained themselves for months for just such an occasion. That act of civil disobedience grounded in prayer and practice, with countless other acts of courage, launched a movement that eventually brought down structures of segregation. It was never going to happen all at once, and, indeed, there's still much work to do. But your prayers and your beliefs matter. They add up to something profound and important. Each prayer and each breakthrough belief is a thread weaving the tapestry of a new reality.

What Would an Apostle Do? Build Your Faith

A coffee mug isn't that big of a deal, but believing like Jesus is. Master the art of wholehearted believing, unhindered by doubt, and you can impact the world more than you could ever have imagined.

As you advance from discipleship to apostleship, doubtless, you will want to ask for bigger things from God than a mug. There are rights to wrong, loaves and fishes to multiply, and wounds to bind up. But start small. Build your faith in your ability to ask and receive. Then visualize the conveyor belt of blessing delivering all kinds of answered prayers and the delight you'll feel when the doorbell rings.

Belief in Action

Beliefs shape your thoughts; thoughts fuel your actions; actions demonstrate your faith, and your faith reinforces your beliefs. So, as you begin to believe *like* Jesus, you will find that you are now able to think new thoughts, take new actions, and develop new faith. Mountains and mulberry trees start to move. The people around you begin to respond in new ways. And the world becomes a brighter place.

- **Believe:** Jesus believes that God hears and answers his prayers. That means Jesus has faith that his prayers have power. He doesn't want to keep that power to himself. Over and over, Jesus tells the Twelve, "Whatever you want, ask for it and believe you have received it." This applies to you as well. Dare to ask, allow, and believe.

- **Answer the Call:** Believe in your prayers as Jesus does. Believe that God has already said "Yes." Then allow God to answer your prayers in God's own way and in God's own time.

- **Practice:** See everything that happens in your life as an answer to a prayer. Perhaps it is an answer to a prayer you don't even remember praying. Focus on what comes your way and what is in front of you. That new opportunity at work. That homemade coffee mug. Those two young heads on a pillow. What have you asked for that is now being answered by the emerging circumstances of your life? Give thanks. Your prayers have power.

The next transformative belief of Jesus builds on the power of your prayer. Turn the page when you are ready to continue your 40-day journey of spiritual transformation.

CHAPTER 6

Believe in a Miracle Mindset

We use the word "miracle" a lot. But what is a miracle, exactly? The dictionary defines it as a surprising and welcome event that can't be explained by natural or scientific laws and, therefore, must be considered the work of divine agency.

Do you know who is pretty good at miracles? Jesus—and his apostles. That is their superpower. No, they don't have a "Spidey" sense, superhuman strength, or the ability to leap tall buildings in a single bound. Rather, their superpower is a miracle mindset. They know that, given their divine partnership with God and the power of their prayers, they can operate in the realm of the miraculous, opening the way for the unexpected to happen. They believe—they know—they can co-create miracles with God.

And you can tap into that superpower, also. If you rise from having faith *in* Jesus to having the faith *of* Jesus, you, too, can co-create miracles with God.

Given the distress much of the world is experiencing today, there is no better time to take this step—to believe like Jesus, to develop the kind of faith Jesus had—so you can actively participate in creating the miracles the world so desperately need right now—at the personal, communal, and societal levels. And let's not forget about the needs of the natural world, and all that impacts it.

To do so, you need to shift the way you see the world. Instead of seeing it as a fixed reality that is simply moving inexorably toward destruction—whether environmental crisis, the breakdown of democracy, the loss of morality, the disappearance of freedoms, the expanding chaos of rapid change, or the breakdown of all that is familiar—it's time to see the world as one string of miracles away from redemption and salvation. This will require a new set of lenses and a literal change of heart. We live in a world that prioritizes head over the heart, the left brain over the right brain, and self-will over God's will. But I say embrace your superpower, believe *like* Jesus, and welcome a miracle mindset into your life. That will empower you to act with creativity and courage, to not give up in quiet resignation. It will change everything.

Jesus' Superpower is Not Performing Miracles but is Believing that He Can

It's easy to think that Jesus' biggest superpower is performing miracles. After all, his miracles are pretty impressive. He changes water into wine, heals the sick, raises the dead, grants sight to the blind, restores peace to the tormented, walks on water, calms wind and waves, and even rises from the dead himself. Everywhere he goes, he is able to heal people. As Matthew reports:

> *Jesus went from there and came to the Sea of Galilee. Then he went up the mountain and sat down. Many people came to Him. They brought with them those who were not able to walk. They brought those who were not able to see. They brought those who were not able to hear or speak and many others. Then they put them at the feet of Jesus and He healed them. All the people wondered. They saw how those who could not*

70

speak were now talking. They saw how those who could not walk were now walking. They saw how those who could not see were now seeing, and they gave thanks to the God of the Jews.

Matthew 15:29-31 (NLV)

Like the people who crowd around Jesus, we wonder where these miracles come from. Jesus isn't bitten by an irradiated spider, as Spiderman was, or sent from an exploding distant planet like Superman; nor is he a brilliant scientist and engineer who could build a flying weaponized suit and become Ironman. Jesus' superpower is his ability to choose faith over doubt, to choose unity with God over disconnection from God, and to choose a mindset that believes all things are possible. When facing the worst of conditions—temptation by Satan, disavowal by family, crucifixion by Pilate—Jesus opts for faith. He isn't swayed by groupthink or done in by peer pressure. Nor is he intimidated by personalities or daunted by principalities. Time and again, he chooses faith in God's future over automatic fears. Drawing on this superpower enables him to stay calm amid conflict, present under pressure, and mindful amid the madness. Being calm, present, and mindful allows him to tune in to God's prompting and have faith in God's plan.

And what results?

All told, there are thirty-six distinct miracle stories in the Gospels.[17] Spaced out, that's one per month for three years. The miracles are a big part of Jesus' ministry on earth. These miracles require his followers to have faith in Jesus to believe he can perform miracles. The miracles also demonstrate the nature of the faith Jesus relies on to create them. The miracles are the message. They show the nearness of the Kingdom of God and express the spiritual power Jesus draws on from God the Father. They also draw others to God.

In the synoptic Gospels[18]—Matthew, Mark, and Luke— miracles are called "deeds of power" from the Greek *dunamis* (sometimes rendered as *dynamis*, the root of "dynamite"). In these Gospels, Jesus draws on the faith of the people to perform these miracles. In the Gospel according to John, miracles are called "signs," from the Greek *semeia*. In John, people develop faith as a result of Jesus' miracles. Either way, it is God who provides the power by which Jesus performs the miracles. Jesus provides the miracle mindset.

Jesus Passes on the Miracle Mindset to the Apostles

The fact that Jesus performed so many miracles tells us how important all four gospel writers think the miracles are. Jesus' miracles aren't only spectacular showpieces to draw people to him—though they certainly do that. Jesus' miracles are how he shows his oneness with God, their partnership, and the power of his prayers. These miracles are a demonstration of the Kingdom of heaven on earth. By passing on the superpower of a miracle mindset to the Twelve, Jesus lets everyone know that his disciples are now apostles named by him to continue this sacred work.

Jesus sends them out not only to spread his message but to perform miracles as well. In this way, the apostles not only show they have faith *in* Jesus, but they also show they have developed the faith *of* Jesus. As apostles, they, too, co-create miracles with God. Through their hands, they multiply loaves and fishes. They cast out demons. They heal the sick. They announce the Kingdom. They make new disciples, baptizing them and teaching them the ways of Jesus. They are no longer simply followers of Jesus but agents of the Kingdom, envoys sent out by Jesus in his name. They now participate in the realm of the miraculous with Jesus.

Embrace the Belief: Use the Miracle Mindset to Activate Your Superpower

Jesus and his apostles aren't the only ones to possess this superpower. God has also given it to you, as shown for example in these New Testament passages:

> *Do not conform to the pattern of this world, but be transformed by the renewing of your mind. Then you will be able to test and approve what God's will is—his good, pleasing and perfect will.*
>
> **Romans 12:2**

> *For the Spirit God gave us does not make us timid, but gives us power, love and self-discipline.*
>
> **2 Timothy 1:7**

These passages confirm the importance of the right mindset—a miracle mindset built on unity and communication with God—in carrying out God's will. God gives us this mindset as a gift of grace, but at the same time, we have to accept it so that we may "be transformed by the renewing of [our] mind." God can give us the mindset to pursue miracles, but we must first believe we can and then go out and do it.

Like Jesus, you, too, have the capacity in every moment to choose your mindset so you can pursue miracles. Don't get me wrong. You'll probably not walk on water the first time out—or ever. But who knows what you can accomplish? After all, Jesus said:

> *Very truly I tell you, whoever believes in me will do the works I have been doing, and they will do even greater things than these, because I am going to the Father. And I will do whatever you ask in my name, so that the*

Father may be glorified in the Son. You may ask me for anything in my name, and I will do it.

John 14:12-14

Cultivating the superpower of a miracle mindset requires a great deal of practice. That's why we're on an extended forty day journey together rather than running a spiritual sprint. The scriptures remind us that even Jesus himself has to grow into wisdom before he can set out into the world. Luke tells the story of Jesus leaving his parents at twelve to learn and teach in the temple. The people are amazed. But when Mary and Joseph frantically track him down, he agrees to go home with them; he isn't ready yet. He still has to grow into his full power. Luke goes on to record the ending of the story: "Then he went down to Nazareth with them and was obedient to them. But his mother treasured all these things in her heart. And Jesus grew in wisdom and stature, and in favor with God and man" (Luke 2:51-52). This maturation process took another eighteen years. According to tradition, he didn't even begin his public ministry until the age of thirty.

Though we call it "mindset," transforming the way you look at the world begins as much in your heart and soul as it does in your mind. To take this step, begin to notice the pattern of your thoughts. Do you tend to paint yourself and the world in a negative or positive light? Ask yourself: Do my thoughts build my faith? Do they make me feel hopeful? Or do they tear me down, turn me toward hopelessness? Only thoughts that build the faith in your heart can lead you to embrace a miracle mindset.

Let's say you're like most of us. Some of your thoughts build you up, and some of them tear you down. How can you shift the balance toward the miraculous? Here are four practical steps to embrace the miracle mindset:

1. Stop complaining.

2. Practice resilience.

3. Choose a growth mindset.

4. Be open to the prompting of the Spirit.

Stop Complaining and Start Thriving

The first step in creating a miracle mindset is to stop complaining. You can't complain and thrive at the same time. Complaining cultivates a negative view of life. It is the opposite of the miracle mindset. Here's what I mean.

Complaining signals to God and your spirit that things aren't good with you, that you are dissatisfied, that things aren't working, and, worse, that they aren't going to work. Complaining is what you do when there is nothing else left to do. But complaining is a dead end. When you complain, you put yourself in victim mode. When you complain, you can't see what else you could be doing to change things. When you complain, you can't see what God is already doing.

Now, let me be clear: lament is different from complaint. Biblically, lament is a powerful tool for navigating hardship. Lament allows us to express deep grief, sorrow, or regret through our words and actions. It can be a cry for help to God, a way to process pain, and ultimately, a path towards finding joy again. Lament acts as a healing balm, giving voice to our deepest emotions and helping us move through them.

I'm not saying you shouldn't lament, nor am I saying don't talk about things that need to be addressed—whether tough family problems or entrenched societal issues. These need to be talked about. Lament—if it doesn't harden into self-pity— leads to solutions.

Complaining, however, is just the opposite. Putting forth a constant stream of negativity, assuming the worst, and badmouthing others simply reinforces the status quo. Complaining all too easily slides into cynicism, which is in direct contrast to a miracle mindset. Cynicism doesn't leave space for miracles to happen. Or for the already miraculous to be noticed.

If, on the other hand, you can program yourself to face even the biggest crisis by being open to the possibility of finding a new way, together with God, you can transform yourself from spiraling downward to soaring upward. In many professional fields, this openness to new ideas and solutions is called innovation. As I noted in *Forging a New Path*, "Crisis leads to innovation."[19] The idea of innovation can be applied to spiritual work as well. Innovation can be a bumpy ride, and change—even positive change—has its ups and downs. But innovation leads to transformation and, ultimately, to a thriving spiritual life.

Recently, a church leader asked me, "If you could do just one thing that leads to innovation, what would it be?" Another leader asked it this way: "If you could do just one thing to help me get ready to change, what would you do?"

"I would adopt a miracle mindset," I responded.

"What do you mean?" they queried.

I explained. "A miracle mindset is what helps us align with Jesus and enter into the consciousness of Jesus. Talk about the miracles. Pray about the miracles. Lift up the miracles. And translate those miracles for the modern world."

One pastor responded, "We're a pretty progressive congregation. We haven't given miracles much thought lately."

Instead, they were trying to reason out what they could do themselves to make things happen. Another commented that she had really lost hope in the God of miracles.

I get it. We lose hope at times. We can be too smart for our own good, getting into our heads rather than our hearts and souls, thinking that if we just work harder, we can get things done and make important changes by a sheer act of will. But we forget that we are not alone. We can tap into our inner divinity and our unity with God to accomplish so much more together than we ever can alone.

I wonder if people who are stuck—even people of good faith—have let that miracle mindset lapse. Most of us wouldn't mind if a miracle or two happened; we just don't orient ourselves toward participating in them. The further away we are from being dream-driven and vision-led, the further away we are from the miracle mindset. I've noticed this in myself and others: we reduce our expectations of ourselves over and over again. Why? So failure is less likely. So we can minimize disappointment and cater to the values of security and safety. The trouble is that spiritual exploration involves risk. There's no getting around that.

The truth is that we rise to the level of expectation we set for ourselves. If we constantly lower expectations, then we have nothing to rise or aspire to. Faith itself is no longer required because nothing is at risk. Predictable processes produce predictable results.

At the same time, we may sense something is missing because life doesn't feel as vital or vibrant when we live in the zone of predictability. Ruts and routines take over. Lowered expectations don't align us with Jesus. He operates in the realm of the miraculous and calls us to rise and join him there.

"What should I do to start this miracle mindset in myself?" one of the same clergy members asked.

"That's great," I affirmed. "You're asking the right questions. Do you really want the answer?"

He nodded a bit uncertainly.

"May I be very direct with you?"

"Yes," he said, still a bit uncertain.

"Stop complaining," I said gently. "Since we started this conversation, all I've heard is a litany of gripes and pet peeves."

Now he looked sheepish, nodding thoughtfully in agreement.

"So change your mindset. Stop complaining. Complaining signals that things aren't good, that you're dissatisfied, that things aren't working, and you doubt they ever will. The trouble with complaining is that it leaves no room for the movement of God and the unfolding miracles around you. It drowns out the very faith you need to move forward."

I don't know exactly what happened with this man after our conversation. What I do know from firsthand experience observing participants in my program called "Creating a Culture of Renewal" is that church leaders often arrive with a predictable set of complaints: we don't have enough money, volunteers, people, new ideas, young people. It's hard to see beyond these circumstances.

I get it. Things can look challenging in the local church these days.

During Creating a Culture of Renewal, however, church leaders discover a more empowering way to approach their mission as we invite them to experience and embrace the miracle mindset. One of the first things they do is create an aspirational covenant with each other about how they will grow together. They hold each other accountable. As they meet month to month, they set their sights on higher ground, and their complaints fall away. We even have monthly "miracle sightings" each time we get together. Before you know it, previously discouraged leaders are recognizing the hand of God at work and miracles all around them. They begin to recognize how their change in perspective actually contributes to the proliferation of miracles.

The bottom line is that a complaining mindset is the opposite of a miracle mindset. So knock it off, friend, and raise your sights higher. Then you, too, will begin to notice the miracles around you.

Practice Resilience

The second way to adopt a miracle mindset is to practice resilience. The quality of resilience is needed more than ever. At this writing, the pandemic, which seems like distant history to many of us, has left behind a path of destruction that has changed the world immeasurably, costing the lives of over a million Americans and changing the economic fortunes of families across the nation and the world. The January 6 attack still echoes in our minds as we wonder if or when the next horrific display of white supremacy and racism will occur. Russia has attacked Ukraine in the kind of war of aggression we thought had ended in the twentieth century. The Middle East is embroiled in a spreading, deadly conflict. For the first time in history, a former President of the United States has been convicted of felonies in a criminal court of law.

It's a very unsettling time. Fear rises to the surface.

When fear threatens to set up camp in your heart, though, remember this: apostles don't panic. Instead, like Jesus, apostles know they have a partnership with God. They know their prayers have power. They know they possess a superpower in their miracle mindset. Buoyed by these divine beliefs, apostles are resilient. They hold a high degree of positive energy and invite others to participate in it. With this miracle mindset, you resist being hijacked by fear and harness your superpowers. Apostles are spiritual badasses in the making. If you don't believe in miracles, you won't see them. If you believe in miracles, you'll see them everywhere, and you'll see how you can participate in bringing them about. So continue to practice resilience—emotional and spiritual.

It was during a time of social and economic disruption that God called me from pastoring churches to what I'm doing now—a ministry of empowering other church leaders and helping to shape the larger conversations in the church. To answer this call, I had to let go of a professional identity, a salary, a parsonage, health insurance, and a supportive community. I had to generate my own practice and bring in my own portfolio of work, all during one of the most precarious times in the first decade of the twenty-first century. This was in the early days of the 2007-2008 economic disaster, when bank failures, a plunging stock market, and a housing crash kicked the economy into a deep recession.

But I did it. I answered the call, and do you know why? Because I realized that I didn't have to cede my faith or surrender my spiritual authority to the storm of world events. Whenever I started to panic, I remembered I could practice resilience and so can you.

Choose a Miracle Mindset

The third way to adopt a miracle mindset is to intentionally choose how you encounter the world—to choose a growth mindset.

A few years back, Stanford professor, psychologist, and researcher Dr. Carol Dweck wrote a groundbreaking book called *Mindset*. Her extensive research revealed two primary mindsets: what she calls a fixed mindset and a growth mindset.[20]

A person with a growth mindset is willing to take chances, enjoys learning new things, and is willing to try hard things they don't know how to do. Those with a growth mindset are not afraid to fail, because failing shows them how to course correct and do something the right way. Conversely, people with fixed mindsets perceive failure as judgment, as revealing the limits of their abilities. They tend to fear learning new things or trying hard things because they don't want to fail at them or risk looking dumb or incompetent.

Everyone is a mix of both fixed and growth mindsets. The crazy thing is that people who are quick to learn as children and praised for qualities such as being naturally smart, naturally pretty, naturally athletic, or a born leader tend toward the fixed mindset. Somewhere deep inside, they think, "What if I try something new and I can't do it? What if I no longer look so smart or pretty or athletic or like a leader?" These folks tend to stay in the known and comfortable zone— their zone of competence—even as they grow up.

I was relieved when I read *Mindset*. It explained some things about myself I hadn't been able to make sense of. As a kid, reading and writing came naturally to me. I was a whiz at spelling. I didn't have to study for tests. You might think

I would have developed a growth mindset because I was so good at things. But in truth, because I was "smart," I didn't know how to try hard because these things came so easily to me. I didn't know how to learn from failure. I didn't know how to apply myself. So when things got hard, as they did in high school and college, I went off and soothed myself with drinking and drugging—better that than risk looking stupid.

Even though I got clean and sober, I still don't want to look stupid. I still sometimes avoid trying new things because—and here's the irony of a fixed mindset—if I don't already know it, I might feel inferior or bad about myself if I can't learn it quickly or well. But then, how do I learn anything new?

That's a fixed mindset. It leads to a dead end.

The good news is that it's never too late to shift from a fixed mindset to a growth mindset. According to Dweck, the way to help people—even as adults—develop a growth mindset is to praise each other not for being smart or a natural at any given activity or concept but for being willing to grow, willing to try, willing to work hard, and yes—and this is so difficult for many of us—willing to fail.

I try to apply this concept in my own life. As a part-time parent of the two little brothers, now four and six years old, I have to constantly catch myself. Instead of saying, "Look how smart you are," I have to remind myself to say, "Look how many different things you tried." Or "Look how you worked hard to figure that out." Or " I'm proud of you for trying something new even though it was hard."

People in a fixed mindset are famous for saying, "We've never done it that way before." They're not dumb. They're not faithless. They are simply used to what is and don't want to risk failing if they change things up too much.

How do we create a growth mindset? Encourage the people in your life to be willing to try and fail, to work hard and puzzle through things, to ask for help when they don't know how to do something, and to have a growth mindset that makes room for miracles in their lives.

Jesus sees the world that way. Not only is he resilient, Jesus has a growth mindset. That's why he can perform miracles. I think the Twelve exemplify the growth mindset also. Jesus regularly puts them in situations to do things they aren't sure how to do—like feeding thousands of people with a few loaves of bread and fish. Or healing people. Or casting out demons. They have to try and fail first before Jesus shows them how to do it the right way. I think it is the very quality of being willing to look dumb or incompetent that is the mark of their faith. It all starts with the call to apostleship: "Come follow me and I will send you out to fish for people" (Mark 1:17).

Be Open to the Prompting of the Spirit

The fourth way to cultivate a miracle mindset is to be open to the prompting of the Holy Spirit. Isaiah 55:8 reminds us to expect the unexpected from God, because God's ways are not our ways: "'For my thoughts are not your thoughts, neither are your ways my ways,' declares the Lord."

It's true! This applies to how God communicates with us as well. One way I know the Spirit is speaking to me is when I get a seemingly random-but-persistent thought. I used to shoo these thoughts away, considering them annoyances. Once I began to pay attention to them, however, I realized God was talking to me through the Spirit, introducing a new thought. I learned to be grateful and act on it.

But not without a few hiccups.

One day, I was doing my favorite task on my to-do list: running errands. I had two stops that day: Staples to buy office supplies and UPS to ship a box.

One thing you have to know about me is that I'm an office supplies nerd. I love to take in the smell of new paper, see endless boxes of pencils and pens, and survey stacks of folders and envelopes. What possibilities come to mind! How productive I'll be once I get all those color-coded file tabs! Surely new sticky notes would help me start my next book! Staples is one of my happy places. Naturally, I decided Staples would be my first stop.

While driving to Staples, I got a gentle prompting: "UPS. Go to UPS first." I tried to ignore it, but the thought kept coming. "UPS. UPS first." I shook it off like a pitcher shaking off a catcher's signal. I wanted to go to Staples first, and by golly, I was going to Staples first.

So I did. I arrived at Staples and wandered through my happy place, breathing in the scent of paper and running my fingers along the rows of binders. Finally, I picked out my purchase—I don't even remember what it was—and headed up front to check out. That's when I noticed the line. It was not just any line; this was the longest line I had ever seen at Staples, except maybe at Christmas. I had no choice but to wait since I was already there. But the longer I waited, the more frustrated I got.

Finally, I made it through the line, paid for whatever it was, and dashed out to the parking lot, where I started up the car and made my way to UPS. When I got there, I had a sinking feeling when I noticed most of the parking spaces in front of the store were empty. I hurried out of the car, ran up to the door, and sure enough, it was locked tight. I was too late to ship my package.

No wonder I had thoughts of UPS. God was trying to help me out. What I thought were random thoughts were actually divine promptings. God has my back, even in the little things. "You should've listened," I chided myself. Nothing is more frustrating than not checking off an item on my to-do list, especially when it's my own doing!

Now I pay closer attention.

What Would an Apostle Do?

The scriptures remind us that when we are faithful in the little things, then God can trust us with the bigger things. Like miracle-making. Do I pay attention now when I get prompts about the order in which to do things? You bet! (Mostly, anyway.) It's also true that when we trust in the little things, we develop trust in God for the bigger things. That deepened trust means we can more easily advance from discipleship to apostleship. When you choose your mindset, uplift your consciousness, and open yourself to the promptings of the Spirit, everything becomes possible. You are now an agent God can use in new ways. You can co-create miracles with God.

Belief in Action

Beliefs shape your thoughts; thoughts fuel your actions; actions demonstrate your faith, and your faith reinforces your beliefs. So, as you begin to believe *like* Jesus, you will find that you are now able to think new thoughts, take new actions, and develop new faith. Mountains and mulberry trees start to move. The people around you begin to respond in new ways. And the world becomes a brighter place.

- **Believe:** With a miracle mindset, God has given him everything and everyone he needs to make the Kingdom dream a reality. Not only does he have unity with God and a deep prayer life, but he also has the Twelve and the Seventy-Two. Even more, Jesus is deeply grateful for all God has endowed him with. Perhaps that is his true source of strength.

  Like Jesus, you, too, can cultivate a deep sense of sufficiency and gratitude, believing that God has endowed you with all you need. Come to love the idea of welcoming the power of believing *like* Jesus, and in no time at all, you will be co-creating miracles with God.

- **Answer the Call:** Now that Jesus has ascended into heaven, we become the hands, feet, and eyes of Christ here on earth as Teresa of Avila, the sixteenth-century Catholic mystic and saint, famously prayed:

  > *Christ has no body but yours,*
  > *No hands, no feet on earth but yours,*
  > *Yours are the eyes with which he looks*
  > *Compassion on this world.*[21]

  Miracles—and a miracle mindset—are as much about perceiving in a different way as they are about some sort of conversion of physical properties. It's about recognizing what's already there in a new way. It's about being "the eyes with which he [Christ] looks / Compassion on this world." You may think God doesn't really need you. That God is all-powerful without you. Not true. God does need you—your energy, your creativity, your willingness. God is waiting to co-create miracles with you.

  Even now, you may think you don't have superpowers. Or that something or someone is missing in your life before you can activate your superpowers. Again, not true. The soul within you is all the proof you need of your inner divinity. That soul, that inner divinity, makes possible everything you are called to do and be and believe. Cultivating an awareness of your inner divinity will actually open up the space for you to see the people God has brought into your life to co-create miracles with you and help you adopt the miracle mindset.

- **Practice:** Learn to see things anew. Wayne Dyer titled one of his books *You'll See It When You Believe It*.[22] Each day, thank God for the gift of life. Thank God for the people and the powers you have in your life. Ask what miracles God would like to co-create with you and believe they will happen. At the same time, treat your mind, body, and spirit with utmost care and love. Practice thinking elevating thoughts. Be as kind to yourself as you would be to others. Cultivate gratitude. Trust that God loves and needs you. This are not selfish practices. Rather, this is about developing a thriving, resilient, growth orientation that is attuned to the Spirit; all necessary to participate with God in the co-creation of miracles.

  Practice looking at the world through the lens of God's grace—through a miracle mindset—and you will be rewarded with the miraculous.

Now that you've seen how the miracle mindset empowers you to have faith *in* Jesus and develop the faith *of* Jesus, it's time to take another step up. Turn to Appendix B, 5 Steps to Co-Creating Miracles with God, at the back of the book, for a creative process to turn the mundane into the miraculous. Or turn the page when you are ready to continue your 40-day journey of spiritual transformation. The next transformative belief of Jesus that you'll learn about builds on a miracle mindset.

CHAPTER 7

Believe Your Life Has Purpose

Jesus believes his divine partnership with God powers his prayers and allows him to lean into his superpower to co-create miracles with God. These transformative beliefs lead to an even greater belief: his life has unwavering purpose directed by God the Father. Jesus lives his life on purpose.

In fact, according to the Gospels, Jesus' life purpose has at least three distinct aspects. The first aspect of Jesus' purpose is that of Savior. Before Mary and Joseph marry, an angel of the Lord speaks to Joseph in a dream about the son Mary will have: "You are to give him the name Jesus, because he will save his people from their sins" (Matthew 1:21). Many Christians read this as a call to wholeness; other Christians believe that Jesus fulfilled the purpose of the Savior when he died on the cross and rose from the dead three days later.

The second aspect of Jesus' purpose is making God's presence widely known. Capernaum is the center of Jesus' public ministry. He spends time there healing the sick, casting out demons, and preaching. Understandably, the good people of Capernaum want him to stick around and heal every last ill they have. But Jesus knows he can't just stay where things are familiar. He has more work to do. Upon hearing their request, "Jesus replied, 'Let us go somewhere else—to the nearby villages—so I can preach there also. That is why I have come.' So he travels throughout Galilee, preaching in their synagogues and driving out demons" (Mark 1:38-39). The Gospel of Luke puts Jesus' response to a similar situation this way: "But he said, 'I must proclaim the good news of the kingdom of God to the other towns also, because that is why I was sent'" (Luke 4:43). Jesus clearly states this aspect of his purpose: "I must proclaim the good news of the kingdom of God"—and not simply to local folks but to everyone he can reach.

The third aspect of Jesus' purpose is testifying to God's truth. The Gospel of John mentions several times that Jesus embodies God's truth: "The Word became flesh and made his dwelling among us. We have seen his glory, the glory of the One and Only who came from the Father, full of grace and truth" (John 1:14). Later Jesus speaks to Pilate in a similar vein: "You say that I am a king. In fact, the reason I was born and came into the world is to testify to the truth. Everyone on the side of truth listens to me" (John 18:37). The truth or *Logos* that Jesus represents is the essential nature of God the Father, and our unity with it.

Jesus directs each aspect of his purpose to the four distinct communities that love and remember him. Each community that captured the stories of Jesus—characterized by the Gospels according to Matthew, Mark, Luke, and John—relates different parts of his life and stresses different purposes. While scholarly opinions vary, its thought that Matthew's Gospel is written to Greek-speaking Jews about Jesus as the Messiah, while Mark's Gospel is for the Gentile church in Rome, and Luke's Gospel is for a more widespread Gentile audience. John's Gospel, on the other hand, was thought to be written to Greek thinkers to persuade them that Jesus was the Christ, emphasizing Jesus as the Truth.

As with Jesus, you may have different purposes for different communities or different times in your life. You may even mean something different to the various people in your life. For example, my dad (and my mom when she was alive) doesn't need me to be a great church leader; he needs me to be a caring daughter. Our foster boys need me to feed them, play with them, and set healthy boundaries; in other words, to be a good mother. The church leaders I work with need me to inspire and challenge them to lead with new skills and courage. Same person, three different purposes.

Jesus Invites You to Live on Purpose

Jesus lived on purpose and called the Twelve to live the same way:

> *As you go, proclaim this message: "The kingdom of heaven has come near. Heal the sick, raise the dead, cleanse those who have leprosy, drive out demons. Freely you have received; freely give."*
> **Matthew 10:7-9**

This is another moment when Jesus promotes the Twelve from disciples to apostles. The Twelve move from witnessing Jesus fulfill his life purpose to taking on that purpose themselves. The actions of the apostles tell us how they elevate themselves, how they rise from having faith *in* Jesus as witnesses and apprentices to having the faith *of* Jesus as agents and apostles.

Now it's your turn.

In this 40 days to spiritual transformation, your invitation is to embrace the belief that, just as Jesus has purpose, you have purpose all your own.

Just as we all have different purposes at different times in our lives, so our lives will reflect different aspects of the Kingdom reality. Your purpose doesn't have to be about ministry per se. In other words, you don't have to be a missionary, a pastor, or an evangelist to live out your life's purpose. Maybe your purpose is to be an entrepreneur, an artist, a bricklayer, a parent, or a preschool teacher. In living his purpose, Jesus shows us how to live our purpose. In experiencing that deep unity with God, using the gift of prayer, and cultivating the miracle mindset, you can live your larger purpose as Jesus did—whatever that purpose may be.

Throughout the New Testament, we see that many people from different walks of life love and emulate Jesus and learn from him. Some give up their old lives and literally trail after him from town to town. Others are sent back into their communities to live their lives in a new and more purposeful way after Jesus heals them. Jesus instructs still others to say nothing about their healing or about him. Regardless, we can imagine that, changed by the presence of Jesus, each person is living according to God's distinct purpose for them.

It's the same for us. While I was called to be a pastor, many of the people I have met along the way have been called to other equally wonderful purposes. They are teachers, golf pros, energy healers, attorneys, parents, athletes, inventors, salesclerks, trainers, oilfield workers, servers, managers, general contractors, law enforcement officers, public servants, and more. When it comes to living life on purpose, it's more about how you live than your job description. This is the Kingdom of God on earth. As quoted by Catholic professor Gil Bailie in his book *Violence Unveiled: Humanity at the Crossroads*, author, philosopher, theologian, educator, and civil rights leader Howard Thurman once said, "Don't ask what the world needs. Ask what makes you come alive, and go do it. Because what the world needs is people who have come alive."[23]

Of course, the opposite can be true as well. Anyone in any role can be inauthentic about their purpose, can be doing what they're doing for all the wrong reasons, for reasons that aren't aligned with Jesus' purpose—out of fear, greed, lust, revenge, a hunger for fame, hubris, envy, and a host of other sins.

To avoid that path, discover what brings you alive and use it to contribute to the joy of Beloved Community. Living on purpose in this way gives you focus. Emboldens you. Protects you against fear. Guides your prayers.

What if you don't know what brings you alive or don't know what your purpose is? I have definitely felt that way. At those times I simply pray: "God, please help me live the deepest purposes of my life." With this prayer, I don't even have to know or decide what my purpose is! I simply follow God's prompting every day, trusting that what comes my way is God's guidance—letting me know my purpose, moment by moment, day by day. In this way, I can trust that I am living every day on purpose.

Jesus' Four Steps to Living on Purpose

It takes resolve to stay on course, to live life on purpose, and to believe fully in that purpose. Setbacks, pushback, fear, and self-doubt can pull you off course. You may wonder how Jesus maintained his capacity to live purposefully amid all the conflict he faced. Let's take another look at the story told in Luke 4:40-44, which I referred to previously. It reveals how Jesus lived his purpose and kept at it despite challenges that threatened to send him off course.

At sunset, the people brought to Jesus all who had various kinds of sickness, and laying his hands on each one, he healed them. Moreover, demons came out of many people, shouting, "You are the Son of God!" But he rebuked them and would not allow them to speak, because they knew he was the Messiah. At daybreak, Jesus went out to a solitary place. The people were looking for him and when they came to where he was, they tried to keep him from leaving them. But he said, "I must proclaim the good news of the kingdom of God to the other towns also, because that is why I was sent." And he kept on preaching in the synagogues of Judea.

To see more clearly how Jesus stays the course, I break down his approach into four steps.

Step One: Do What You Love

In this story, Jesus is laying hands on people who are sick and ailing—physically and spiritually. He heals them and casts out the demons that are tormenting them. He is clearly in his element, doing what he loves and doing it well. Perhaps that is the first step to living on purpose—enjoying your life and work.

Now consider: What deeply engages you, fruitfully uses your gifts, is natural for you, and serves the greater good? Doing what you love needn't be considered self-indulgent. Rather, it is a sign that you are using your God-given gifts.

As you use your gifts, they will lead you to deepen your purpose. Maybe you're an inspiring, persuasive speaker or a great event planner or you have a way with kids or teenagers. Trust that using these skills is living your purpose.

At the same time, be open to the new ways God may be prompting you to use your gifts. In the days before I went to seminary, for example, I sold newspaper advertising and motivational cassette tapes. I was using my gifts. I loved meeting new people, believed in my products, wanted to help businesses grow, and loved to help empower people. There was nothing wrong with what I was doing—I enjoyed it and did it well—but later, I would be prompted to see that God wanted me to use these same gifts in a different way, in a different setting.

Step Two: Address Challenges that Arise

As Jesus helps people, challenges arise. Demons have to be dealt with, as do competing claims on his time and competing visions for his life. The people Jesus heals beg him to stay. Everywhere Jesus goes, they want more of him. Understandably, they don't want him to leave. He has changed their lives! But that doesn't mean they have any special claim on him.

Jesus' challenge is to stay the course and stay true to his core values. He does this by facing challenges as they arise. He doesn't avoid them or pretend they don't exist. He speaks directly to them.

Now consider your own life. What pulls you off course or causes you to settle for a lesser good when you run into a challenge that threatens your larger purpose?

Step Three: Be Clear About Your Purpose

In this Gospel story, Jesus answers the people begging him to stay by pushing back and setting boundaries: "I must proclaim the good news of the kingdom of God to the other towns also, because that is why I was sent." To paraphrase, Jesus is saying: I have to keep moving. I have other places to go and people to heal, to fulfill my God-given purpose.

As you face the challenges that arise, you too will need to clarify your higher purpose. Even though mustering this level of clarity or setting these kinds of boundaries can feel awkward or uncomfortable, it's critical to do so to maintain your integrity. Pastors who work seventy to eighty hours a week in an attempt to show how much they love and support their congregations, for example, often sacrifice their own family life and miss out on important events that mean the world to their spouse or children. Be clear with yourself and others so your life is lived on purpose, in alignment with your core values, not merely as an exercise of duty and obligation. It takes courage to be clear. But it's worth it.

Step Four: Let Purpose Lead the Way

Jesus is clear with himself and the people around him. As a result, he is able to stay on course: "He kept on preaching in the synagogues of Judea." He understood his purpose, communicated it firmly and clearly, and didn't let challenges stop him. Once clarity about your true purpose emerges you know what to do next. Rely on your purpose to lead the way.

Embrace the Belief: Your Life Has Purpose

To embrace the belief that your life has purpose, personalize the process by writing out these steps:

1. List what comes naturally and easily to you and serves a greater good. What are your gifts, skills, and talents? What are your resources? What brings you joy?

2. Note any challenges that arise as you use these gifts to accomplish your purpose. How can you address them?

3. Reflect on how these challenges push you to clarify what you really want and need to do. How can you be clear about your purpose with others?

4. Where is your purpose leading you next?

What Would an Apostle Do?

Advancing from discipleship to apostleship means saying YES to opportunities, requests, and needs consistent with your gifts, skills, and life's purpose.

But don't worry if you are not crystal clear on your purpose right away. I remember when I was agonizing over my call to the ministry. I was in my second year in seminary. I had landed there via a divine prompting. All my classmates seemed to know what they were doing there, but I didn't. Should I become a social worker? A chaplain? An academic? Something else? After all, I hadn't been raised in the church, and the whole Christian life was new. I had already tried to wriggle out of becoming a Christian, but Jesus wouldn't let me do that. One night, I simply asked Jesus into my heart, and it was a done deal.

But for sure, I wasn't going to be a minister. That much I knew. That seemed too much of a stretch for me.

I lost that fight, too.

One day in my second year of seminary, sitting in the back row of Church History class, I sensed God calling me. I heard him say, "Minister to my people." I knew from the context—seminary—that God meant his Christian people. That's all I knew—that God wanted me to minister to his Christian people. He didn't give me much else in the way of details.

I wrestled mightily with this sense of calling. I felt like it meant leaving my Jewish community and identity behind and striking out in a whole new direction. I couldn't seem to find peace with this prospect. Trying to figure it out was agonizing. Thankfully, God later showed me how to integrate both my Jewish and Christian identities. One day, a sense of peace and calm descended on me, an epiphany. My gifts were my path. God wouldn't call me to a path I wasn't prepared for.

And what were my gifts? Not only the skills from my sales career but also writing, speaking to groups, and getting people organized. While in seminary, I received positive comments on services I had designed and sermons I had written and delivered. That these were my gifts was confirmed when a man named Harvey Martz came through the receiving line at the Iliff School of Theology after one of those services I had helped design and sermons I had preached. He stuck out his hand, introduced himself as the Chair of the Board of Ordained Ministry, and said something to the effect of, "We'd like to have you." As quickly as that, I knew becoming a pastor of a congregation was the right path for me. Just as Jesus' purpose was revealed in his gifts, so too was mine. And so will your purpose be revealed to you.

If all else fails, simply act as though you do have purpose and that what you are currently involved in reveals some aspect of your purposeful life. After all, "All things work together for the good for those who love the Lord and are called according to God's purpose" (Romans 8:28). If you make God's purpose your purpose, you can't go wrong.

Belief in Action

Beliefs shape your thoughts; thoughts fuel your actions; actions demonstrate your faith, and your faith reinforces your beliefs. So, as you begin to believe *like* Jesus, you will find that you are now able to think new thoughts, take new actions, and develop new faith. Mountains and mulberry trees start to move. The people around you begin to respond in new ways. And the world becomes a brighter place.

- **Believe:** Jesus has faith in his life purpose; he believes in that purpose: "to proclaim the good news of the kingdom of God ... that is why I was sent." Believe *like* Jesus. Seek your life purpose, and once you find it, believe in it like Jesus did. Live on purpose.

- **Answer the Call:** Sometimes, the hardest part of living on purpose isn't finding your purpose but accepting it. You may have put all kinds of roadblocks in your way to keep from accepting your purpose. Maybe accepting your purpose requires a huge life change you don't think you're ready for. Maybe it requires an investment in time and money that might stretch you thin. Maybe your true purpose doesn't come with the status, acclaim, or remuneration you're used to. But when you know God's purpose for you, you *know*, and it's best not to turn and run. Jonah tried that and look how that worked out for him—three days in a whale's belly. Answer God's invitation to live life on purpose. And if you still don't know your purpose? That's okay, too. Fake it until you make it. Act with good intentions as if you have found your purpose, even if you don't know exactly what it is yet. It will find you. I promise you.

- **Practice:** If you know your purpose, that's great. Practice believing in it every day. Do something toward your greater purpose every day. Better yet, create a mindfulness that everything you do every day contributes to God's purpose for you. If you're cooking dinner for your family, do it with the knowledge that that's part of God's purpose. Do it with a higher consciousness. Do it with prayerfulness. The same goes for mowing the lawn, doing laundry, or baking cookies for the classroom fundraiser. None of these have the pizazz of healing the sick or casting out demons, but they all matter; they all contribute if done while believing *like* Jesus. Everything you do, if you do it in good faith and if you do it with the faith *of* Jesus, is part of your larger purpose. Believe that each thing that happens each day has a purpose and act that way. With the grace of God, it does.

Purposeful living prepares you for the final transformative belief of Jesus. Turn the page when you are ready to continue your 40-day journey of spiritual transformation.

CHAPTER 8

Believe that Resurrection Is Real

Of all the stories in the New Testament, the most consistently reported are the crucifixion and resurrection. Graphic accounts of both appear in all four Gospels, although details vary. But with one voice, the gospel writers agree: crucifixion is a cruel and heartbreaking end to Jesus, to this miracle-maker, this teacher of love and transformation. It's a terribly unjust ending to this just, godly person. And yet, this horror is followed by the most inexplicable of miracles—the miracle of resurrection.

Just as the accounts of crucifixion vary in each Gospel, so do the details of the resurrection. Yet, with one voice, the gospel writers agree on one more thing: Jesus seems to know resurrection is coming. He confides in the Twelve ahead of the crucifixion that things are going to get very dark, but after that, light will dawn again. Jesus tells them, "The Son of Man is going to be delivered into the hands of men. They will kill him, and after three days he will rise" (Mark 9:31). "After three days he will rise"—the very essence of possibility. A dead end turns into a new beginning.

Not only does Jesus believe in the reality of resurrection for himself, but he also believes in it for others.

Consider the story of Jesus raising Lazarus from the dead.

Martha and Mary, friends of Jesus and sisters of Lazarus, send word to Jesus to come quickly so he can heal their brother, who is very sick. Jesus loves this family, yet he delays. On purpose. In fact, Jesus waits long enough before setting out that by the time he and his friends leave for Bethany, Lazarus has already died. Jesus tells the disciples, "Lazarus has died, and for your sake I am glad that I was not there, so that you may believe. But let us go to him" (John 11:14b-15). When Jesus arrives, the sisters are heartbroken and maybe angry. Jesus tells Martha, "Your brother will rise again." She affirms the resurrection conceptually. Martha said to him, "I know that he will rise again in the resurrection on the last day" (John 11:24). Yet, Jesus provides resurrection in an immediate way.

> *Then Jesus, deeply moved again, came to the tomb. It was a cave, and a stone lay against it. Jesus said, "Take away the stone." Martha, the sister of the dead man, said to him, "Lord, by this time there will be an odor, for he has been dead four days." Jesus asked her, "Did I not tell you that if you believed you would see the glory of God?" So they took away the stone. And Jesus lifted up his eyes and said, "Father, I thank you that you have heard me. I knew that you always hear me, but I said this on account of the people standing around, that they may believe that you sent me." When he had said these things, he cried out with a loud voice, "Lazarus, come out." The man who had died came out, his hands and feet bound with linen strips, and his face wrapped with a cloth. Jesus said to them, "Unbind him, and let him go."*
> **John 11:38-44**

We see from this story that resurrection is not an isolated act. It has tremendous impacts on those who witness it. Imagine the faith that Martha and Mary come to have, watching their brother be resurrected. Imagine the faith that

Lazarus must now have, having personally experienced both death and resurrection. Mind-boggling.

The same is true of the Twelve. Before the crucifixion, Jesus tells his apostles that, even though they will scatter once he is taken and killed, he will still be there for them and bring them back together. "But after I have risen, I will go ahead of you into Galilee" (Mark 14:28). Indeed, Jesus meets them on the path as they head back to Galilee after the terrible events of the crucifixion in Jerusalem. They aren't alone, after all. Jesus is with them again, still leading them, guiding them, teaching them. Jesus' resurrection provides them with deep hope and guidance.

Sometimes, it seems that life hands us dead ends. Bleakness is all that lies before us. While things are bound to be better in heaven, what about life now? How are we to go on in situations like these?

We have much to learn from Jesus. Faced with the worst of dead-end circumstances—an unjust death by crucifixion— Jesus feels dread and moves forward anyway. He trusts his faith more than he gives in to automatic fears. In Gethsemane, he knows what is coming, the agonies he will suffer, and yet he surrenders to what lies ahead. "He withdrew about a stone's throw beyond them, knelt down and prayed, 'Father, if you are willing, take this cup from me; yet not my will, but yours be done'" (Luke 22:41-42). Jesus believes in the reality of resurrection and puts that belief ahead of his fears. It's not that he discounts the pain that awaits him. He doesn't. Instead, he chooses to trust God in the worst moments of his life.

Martha knows, too, that a new ending is possible for her brother, even after he has been dead for four days. Only by believing in the reality of resurrection as Jesus does can we work through our own fears—about who we are, the future, the value of life, and faith itself.

Resurrection can seem elusive. Yes, we know Jesus rose from the dead. It's a great story—whether you take it literally or figuratively. Yet, how many of us expect to rise from the dead in this life—to have things unexpectedly or even miraculously work out? Fear has a sort of irresistible allure. It sometimes seems a safer bet to catastrophize, to believe in a fearful outcome, than to place our faith in a positive future. Catastrophizing is a common human phenomenon. As I mentioned earlier, it's part of the brain being hardwired for survival and caution. Even so, we are not stuck with our instincts. We can rise above them to embrace the reality of resurrection. So let's take a closer look at fear and see it for what it really is.

When we give in to our F.E.A.R., we create the mindset of "Future Events Already Ruined." We become Negative Nellies. We expect things to turn out badly. Negativity slams the door shut. Sure, you may stay somewhat safe behind closed doors, but at what cost?

The story is told that the disciples go into hiding after the crucifixion. They barricade their doors and lay low out of fear (John 20:19). All they can imagine are the worst possible outcomes.

We do the same thing. When things are going bad, it's hard to imagine anything but more bad coming our way. But this hiding out in future events already ruined comes at a cost: the cost of growth, the cost of all the beliefs we are trying to accept when we transform ourselves to believe *like* Jesus: to believe in our partnership with God, the power of our prayer, a miracle mindset, living on purpose, and, of course, the reality of resurrection. We won't find any of these behind a shut door. To believe in the reality of resurrection is to allow good things to happen, to open the door for good things to enter.

Let me propose a way to turn fear around. It's all about transforming your mindset. You can create a different mindset about the future if you ascribe a different meaning to the acronym. F.E.A.R. can just as easily stand for "Forgetting Everything's All Right." Or even better: "Face Everything and Rise." That's the opposite of negative, the opposite of defeatist. Putting it that way opens the door—opens our minds, hearts, and souls—to God's grace, to believe *like* Jesus. Jesus was anything but defeatist. He has faith in the rock-solid knowledge that all things are possible with God. That's what the resurrection is all about.

What Would an Apostle Do?

To believe *like* Jesus in the reality of resurrection, we must face our fears, both our micro fears about our own worthiness to receive God's grace and our macro fears for the world at large. We must resist the temptation to indulge in self-pity—I'm not good enough, I'm not rich enough, I'm not strong enough, I'm not smart enough, it's too late for me. Regarding the big picture, we must resist the temptation to "doom scroll" the internet or obsessively watch the news on TV. I'm not saying you shouldn't be informed, but you've probably noticed that in a 24/7 news cycle, news stories are repeated ad nauseum. Checking in once or twice a day—or even several times a week—should do the trick.

Now is the time to up your faith in a positive future. Yes, bad things happen. Jesus is tried and, in a parody of justice, crucified. But he is also resurrected. What opens more possibilities for us than that? The Lord is risen. Worldly powers do not have the final say. When we believe *like* Jesus, have the faith *of* Jesus, and step into that faith to co-create miracles with God, we not only rise again, but we have the privilege of making the world a better place for all. If you think about it this way, what's to fear? Jesus has already shown us the way.

My beautiful mom, Dotty, was diagnosed with ALS (amyotrophic lateral sclerosis), also known as Lou Gehrig's disease, at the age of eighty. She lived with ALS for more than seven years until she recently passed away, several months shy of eighty-eight. During that time, she embodied beauty, grace, and resilience, even when this cruel disease robbed her of speech, movement, laughter, and tears.

The last seven years with Mom was a long haul. I wouldn't wish ALS on anyone. It only advances, never retreats. It's the ultimate dead end, the ultimate unjust death. The average life expectancy after diagnosis is two to five years. Yet, embraced by my father, who fully lived his wedding vows of self-sacrificing love through thick and thin, exquisitely cared for by a lively and engaged team of round-the-clock caregivers, and dearly loved by all of her five children, their spouses and kids, as well as her brothers, my mom lived an extraordinarily full life and outlasted all expectations. Even when my mom was confined to a wheelchair, and long after she could no longer enjoy the pleasure of eating, but instead had to receive nutrition through a feeding tube, my mom and dad found ways to enjoy life. On Saturdays, a fun-loving caregiver would take my mom out to the movies. Another caregiver helped my mom shop for new clothes online. My mom and dad continued to attend the opera once a month. My dad insisted we all look past the immobilizing disease to the beautiful, living, loving human being still inside a body that was breaking down.

As tough as the last seven years were, much good came out of it as well. No, my mom didn't miraculously rise from her wheelchair and begin to walk and talk again. Nor did she rise from the dead after she took her last breath. But I watched the most extraordinary resurrections happen in other ways in our family.

From the beginning, my dad made an extraordinary commitment to my mom to devote himself to her well-being so she would have the best possible life for as long as she lived. My father's love meant my mother didn't have to face her disease alone.

Following our father's example, after my mom was diagnosed, all of us siblings and our spouses started visiting our parents more often. We didn't want Dad to feel alone either. We'd take turns chatting with Mom—though, after a while, she couldn't really answer—and hanging out with Dad. Seeing their love and courage made us all want to be better people and brought us closer together.

Even the pandemic shutdowns several years later didn't stop us. We simply met weekly online, which had the unexpected benefit of expanding our initially small circle of support to include far-flung family members who wouldn't have otherwise been able to join us. My mom's extended family and my dad's became part of our regular meetings, including my dad's youngest brother, who had been somewhat estranged from the family for years. Now reconnected and reconciled, this fun and interesting uncle contributes to our weekly family meetings. Through these regular family gatherings, we have strengthened our family bonds. Because of this newfound closeness, when my mom's illness progressed to the point where we needed to make tough decisions, all of us kids were able to work well together, collaborating on her care and expressing courtesy and respect to each other even when we didn't see eye to eye. In addition to the larger family meetings, we had online sibling meetings to share information, exchange ideas, and make decisions.

The morning my mom transitioned, we knew what to do. All of us siblings immediately gathered online to figure out when and where the service would be held, how it would be conducted, and the myriad details that needed to be decided even when you think you have the plans all in place. Everyone pitched in. When conflicts arose, we found ways to work through them.

Three days later, we met in the Connecticut town we were raised in to lay my mom to rest in a hillside cemetery. Family members flew in from far-off places. The team of caregivers traveled with us to the service, included as family. Siblings stepped up to offer extra hospitality to those who needed it. A webcam livestreamed the service for those who couldn't travel.

In honor of the Jewish faith my parents raised us with and that continued to give my mom solace throughout her life, we followed the direction of the cantor who led the graveside service, tearing a piece of black cloth to symbolize our grief and shoveling dirt ourselves onto the plain wooden casket adorned with a simple star of David. We sat shiva for several days, receiving guests, reciting prayers, and eating lox and bagels.

The day we were all to leave Connecticut and go our separate ways, my dad said, "We can't just bury your mom and be done with her." There and then, we made a commitment to meet online the next morning to once again recite the Mourner's Kaddish, the Jewish prayer said by those who have lost a dear loved one. Children say it for their parents daily for one year. It helps get through the period of most intense grief.

We met for Kaddish for one day, then one week, then one month, and three months later we are still going strong. We have quietly decided to meet together for the full year. Our meetings last about twenty minutes, but this closeness and connection and care for my dad are nothing short of miraculous—a true resurrection. Our family didn't have this kind of closeness before my mom got sick. As heartbroken as my dad is after losing his wife of sixty-seven years, he is stronger than expected. The ritual is helping us all grieve, learn more about the mom we loved, honor and explore our Jewish heritage, and surprisingly, reveal new beliefs in God for some of the family members. Caregivers, cousins, nephews, and nieces attend the morning meetings from time to time to join us in this resurrection journey of grief.

With this experience, I can tell you that I believe even more deeply in the reality of resurrection. Even though my mom wasn't miraculously healed, nor was a cure for ALS found before she died—and to add insult to injury, it was discovered that she had stage four cancer a few weeks before she died— still something else has risen from her bleak circumstances that I never could have predicted. Her spirit is more alive and well in us than we ever could have expected. The family she left behind is more fully connected than we would have been had she not gotten sick. New family relationships have developed, and my eighty-eight-year-old dad is finding his footing again. Resurrection is real, even when it doesn't look like you think it will or hope it will.

My family is living proof that when you think you've hit a dead end and the world seems hopeless, there are still possibilities beyond what you can see. This isn't the time to give up hope in God or yourself or the people around you. People will rise up and surprise you!

Embrace the Belief: DARE to Dream

As your soul makes room for this new level of belief in possibility and resurrection, use the DARE model to embrace and embody this, as well as Jesus' other four beliefs. Adapted from my book *Dream Like Jesus*, this four-step model invites you to use your holy imagination to call something new into being.

DREAM

Begin to dream now of what a resurrected reality would look like. Focus on your future faith, gratitudes, and family life, and think about what you would like to contribute to your loved ones, your church, your community, and the world around you. Volunteering? Mentoring? Leadership? Maybe you'll even consider changing your life to make your contributions more formal or professional. Allow the Holy Spirit to shape your vision and guide your thoughts. This is an important step in daring to dream and believe *like* Jesus.

ALIGN

Bring yourself into alignment with God by receiving and welcoming divine courage, comfort, and confidence to envision the reality of resurrection. Allow your beliefs to shift so that you can naturally align with this positive vision. Then invite others into your dream of a new future by sharing it out loud. Alan Layman, a participant in Creating a Culture of Renewal—a program I developed to empower faith leaders to advance from discipleship to apostleship—did just that.

Deeply disturbed at the homelessness impacting families in his Virginia community, he and a vision team conceived a bold, inspiring dream to restore dignity and safety: "Every family in Chester, Virginia has a stable, secure home."

On a Tuesday, Alan and I met with a group of other leaders from Creating a Culture of Renewal, who were each declaring their dream out loud in preparation for the year ahead. On Wednesday, the next day, Alan sent me an email with the subject line: "A Miracle!" In the email, he explained to me how, after we had met, he met with his board, where he shared a little of his vision for Trinity United Methodist Church and the Chester community.

"This morning," he wrote, "one of the members of the Board informed me that he and his wife intend to give $100,000 to 'The Dream Like Jesus.' At first, I was speechless, now I can't stop crying. Mercy."

Mercy, indeed! Alan's email affirmed to me that others want to believe in the reality of resurrection, too. They are eager to join you in believing *like* Jesus.

REALIZE

Now that you have envisioned the reality of resurrection and are aligning your soul and beliefs with that vision, let God guide you into realizing this new reality. Is there an action for you to take? A person to have a conversation with? Watch how God brings unexpected people and situations into your life. Like Alan found, the changes may come about faster than you ever imagined! We are hungry for bravery, hungry for solutions, hungry for a brighter world. We are hungry to put our faith into action. When we open ourselves to believe *like* Jesus, we can find new ways of being and doing in an ever-changing world.

113

We can co-create wondrous miracles with God.

EXPAND

As you develop the faith *of* Jesus and come to believe in the reality of resurrection, the miracles you and God co-create will expand far beyond you. This kind of faith is contagious! Others will want to participate in your excitement, resilience, faith, hopefulness, and forward motion. They will want to join you in the good you are doing. Watch how one daring dream expands into others when nurtured with possibility. Spirits rise, buoyed on the life-giving current of possibility.

Belief in Action

Beliefs shape your thoughts; thoughts fuel your actions; actions demonstrate your faith, and your faith reinforces your beliefs. So, as you begin to believe *like* Jesus, you will find that you are now able to think new thoughts, take new actions, and develop new faith. Mountains and mulberry trees start to move. The people around you begin to respond in new ways. And the world becomes a brighter place.

- **Believe:** Believe in the reality of resurrection by placing more faith in God's positive future than in your fear. If you have faith in the possibilities of the future, you don't need evidence that good things will happen. Your choice to believe *like* Jesus is all the proof you need.

- **Answer the Call:** Answer the call of possibility, of belief in resurrection. That doesn't mean you won't have doubts from time to time, or that you won't have fears. As Rooster Cogburn in the 1969 movie *True Grit*, John Wayne famously said, "Courage is being scared to death and saddling up anyway." That's as good a mantra for an apostle as any. Courage is being scared to death and having the faith of Jesus anyway. Don't pretend you have no fear, but turn that fear around. Don't let it shut you down. Instead, use it as fuel.

- **Practice:** A friend of mine used to say, "It ain't over till it's over, and if it ain't good, then it ain't over." Develop the practice of looking for the good in each situation. Amplify it. Write about it. Talk about it. Lift it up. Rename your problems as opportunities and act as such. I don't want to make light of it, but Jesus can see beyond the horror of crucifixion to the good that lay beyond it. He isn't naïve, nor does he ask us to discount our own pain. Rather, Jesus invites us to see the good that comes out of even the worst of circumstances, like the deep family connections that have resulted from my mother's ALS.

Now that we have explored the five transformative beliefs of Jesus, it is time to put these beliefs into practice in your own life. Turn the page when you are ready to continue your 40-day journey of spiritual transformation.

Part 3

The Journey Continues: Putting the Faith *of* Jesus to Work in Your Life

So far in your 40-day journey, you've discovered the five beliefs of Jesus and adopted them into your life as the foundation and inspiration for believing *like* Jesus in order to rise from disciple to apostle. Now it's time to find out what's next: how to *live* like an apostle.

CHAPTER 9

Water-Walking Faith

Today's Christians need a new focus, even as the wider world needs new hope. Our faith has been hijacked by conflict in the institutional church and by new challenges posed by social and political polarization. We've put our energy into choosing sides against each other rather than coalescing under the call to take on the faith *of* Jesus, to believe *like* Jesus. The world needs people brave enough to transcend the politics of grievance and dogged enough to see past endless litanies of complaint to envision a new, more positive world. Now is the time to come together and take the next steps in following the way of Jesus: shifting from a focus on belief *in* Jesus toward rising together to believe *like* Jesus.

Taking on the belief *of* Jesus requires advancing from discipleship to apostleship. As you do, you expand both your consciousness and your capacities to be ever more Christ-like. Apostleship is what Christians are meant to do. It's who Christians are meant to be.

Apostolic Christians are poised to be the kind of Christians to whom Jesus once said, "All authority in heaven and on earth has been given to me. Therefore go and make disciples of all nations, baptizing them in the name of the Father and of the Son and of the Holy Spirit, and teaching them to obey everything I have commanded you. And surely I am with you always, to the very end of the age" (Matthew 28:18-20). By making new disciples, we are adding to the cadre of soon-to-be miracle-makers that Jesus began raising up.

To truly believe *like* Jesus and embody the faith *of* Jesus, you have to get inside his head. Fortunately, there's a good record of how he thought about things: the parables and stories collected in the Gospels of the New Testament. One of Jesus' constant themes is the matter of faith and belief. Both the upside of having it and the downside of not having it.

Jesus knows that faith is a powerful thing. That's why he calls the Twelve and the Seventy-Two to persist in their faith. Among his most pointed comments are to call someone "faithless" or to say, "O, you of little faith." To step into the fullness of faith and truly activate our faith, we have to believe *like* Jesus does. To believe *like* Jesus means tapping into the same source of power and field of energy he does. To do that, we need to develop a new spiritual consciousness, create a new mindset, and undergo a spiritual transformation. The same kind of transformation Jesus has undergone.

We cannot do the things Jesus does, experience our own oneness with God, or tap into our God-given agency if we keep our old mindset. These things are simply not compatible with each other. We must advance from discipleship to apostleship. We must see the world in a brand-new way, through Jesus' eyes, with Jesus' faith.

Jesus makes it clear that he wants us to have the same kind of faith he has. But, it isn't easy. It takes a lot of practice. Even then, the disciples don't always get it right at first. Take the story of Peter attempting to walk on the water in Matthew 14:22-33:

Immediately Jesus made the disciples get into the boat and go on ahead of him to the other side, while he dismissed the crowd. After he had dismissed them, he went up on a mountainside by himself to pray. Later that night, he was there alone, and the boat was already a considerable distance from land, buffeted by the waves because the wind was against it.

Shortly before dawn Jesus went out to them, walking on the lake. When the disciples saw him walking on the lake, they were terrified. "It's a ghost," they said, and cried out in fear.

But Jesus immediately said to them: "Take courage! It is I. Don't be afraid."

"Lord, if it's you," Peter replied, "tell me to come to you on the water."

"Come," he said.

Then Peter got down out of the boat, walked on the water and came toward Jesus. But when he saw the wind, he was afraid and, beginning to sink, cried out, "Lord, save me!"

Immediately Jesus reached out his hand and caught him. "You of little faith," he said, "why did you doubt?"

And when they climbed into the boat, the wind died down. Then those who were in the boat worshiped him, saying, "Truly you are the Son of God."

A lot is going on in this story. After dismissing the crowd he was preaching to, Jesus walked on the water to catch up with the disciples, who had gone ahead of him in a boat to get to the other side of the Sea of Galilee. The disciples see a figure approaching them on the water, but at first, they don't think it's Jesus. They think it's some kind of ghost or apparition. At this point, they don't even have full faith *in* Jesus. They don't believe Jesus can water-walk until Jesus assures them that it is indeed him.

121

That's when Peter gets into the act and exercises the growth mindset by trying something new and hard. He says if it is Jesus and not a ghost, then Jesus should call him out onto the water, too. Jesus agrees. Peter swings his leg over the side of the boat and places one foot first and then the other on the water. Miraculously, the water holds firm under his feet. He takes some tentative steps on the water and manifests water-walking faith.

But this expansive faith doesn't last long. It's fleeting. When the wind kicks up, Peter loses focus, gets scared, doubts his abilities, and stops believing *like* Jesus, feeling the pull of gravity. Peter starts to sink, begging Jesus to save him. Jesus, of course, reaches out to Peter and gets him safely back into the boat.

Even with a growth mindset, Peter could not sustain the faith *of* Jesus. He and the others haven't undergone the spiritual growth to fully adopt Jesus' faith and beliefs. In fact, it is only after Jesus saves Peter that the disciples in the boat, including Peter, recognize Jesus as the Son of God. They needed greater proof to support their faith. But when you think about it, Peter had all the proof he needed. After all, he was walking on water! He got exactly what he prayed for, but he got into his head, as many of us do, and couldn't fully embrace what was happening, so he pushed it away.

That's the lesson for the disciples here—and for us. Jesus wants us to open ourselves to the possibility of expanding our faith to welcome and integrate new beliefs. "You of little faith!" Jesus says when Peter begins to go under. "Why did you doubt?" What exactly is it that Peter doubts? I don't think Peter is doubting Jesus. Rather, I think Peter is doubting himself and his ability to believe and act like Jesus. Jesus wants Peter to take on the same faith Jesus has, the kind of faith that allows Jesus to traverse the seas on foot. This is the faith *of* Jesus, which, if Peter had sustained it, would have allowed him to act just like Jesus—in this case, walk on water with confidence and ease, even in windy weather. Peter has yet to fully embrace this water-walking faith.

Belief and Disbelief

What happens when you can't muster water-walking faith? When you want to, but, like Peter, doubt dogs you? Consider the conversation between Jesus and the father of a possessed boy in Mark 9:14-29. It all centers on belief.

Amid a large crowd, Jesus encounters the father of a boy who is possessed by a spirit. The boy might have had something like epilepsy. He experiences convulsions and foaming at the mouth. During these episodes, the boy becomes rigid and is unable to speak.

> *When they came to the other disciples, they saw a large crowd around them and the teachers of the law arguing with them. As soon as all the people saw Jesus, they were overwhelmed with wonder and ran to greet him.*
>
> *"What are you arguing with them about?" he asked.*
>
> *A man in the crowd answered, "Teacher, I brought you my son, who is possessed by a spirit that has robbed him of speech. Whenever it seizes him, it throws him to the ground. He foams at the mouth, gnashes his teeth and becomes rigid. I asked your disciples to drive out the spirit, but they could not."*
>
> *"You unbelieving generation," Jesus replied, "how long shall I stay with you? How long shall I put up with you? Bring the boy to me."*
>
> *So they brought him. When the spirit saw Jesus, it immediately threw the boy into a convulsion. He fell to the ground and rolled around, foaming at the mouth.*

Jesus asked the boy's father, "How long has he been like this?"

"From childhood," he answered. "It has often thrown him into fire or water to kill him. But if you can do anything, take pity on us and help us."

"If you can?" said Jesus. "Everything is possible for one who believes."

Immediately the boy's father exclaimed, "I do believe; help me overcome my unbelief!"

When Jesus saw that a crowd was running to the scene, he rebuked the impure spirit. "You deaf and mute spirit," he said, "I command you, come out of him and never enter him again."

The spirit shrieked, convulsed him violently and came out. The boy looked so much like a corpse that many said, "He's dead." But Jesus took him by the hand and lifted him to his feet, and he stood up.

After Jesus had gone indoors, his disciples asked him privately, "Why couldn't we drive it out?"

He replied, "This kind can come out only by prayer."

This story is a fascinating examination of faith. Jesus has faith. He is "one who believes." The boy's father, too, has a kind of faith. He is both "one who believes" and one who disbelieves. But here the disciples seem to be lacking in faith altogether. "I asked your disciples to cast it out," the boy's father says, speaking of the deaf and mute spirit that has gripped his son since childhood, "and they were not able." Why is it that the disciples seem to be lacking in the kind of faith needed to rebuke and command this unclean spirit? "This kind can only come out by prayer," Jesus instructs them. Though they tried to drive out the impure spirit, apparently they still lacked Jesus' kind of belief in the power of prayer.

After bemoaning their lack of faith, Jesus casts out the unclean spirit and heals the boy. Later, when the disciples ask why they couldn't do the same, Jesus teaches them what was missing. Their apostolic training continues, as does their growth mindset.

In the meantime, Jesus answers the father's prayer despite the father's somewhat contradictory plea: "I do believe; help me overcome my unbelief!" One way of interpreting this line is that the father sincerely wants to believe and thinks he does believe, but he isn't fully there yet. As such, the father echoes Peter's "Lord save me!" when he finds himself floundering in the sea.

Both Peter and the father are stand-ins for all of us who want to believe, who think we believe but, like the father in the parable and the disciples, haven't fully embraced the transformative nature of our faith. We haven't fully come to water-walking faith, or embraced all that is possible.

What is water-walking faith, exactly? Quite simply, water-walking faith is the faith *of* Jesus. It is believing *like* Jesus.

As we take this transformational journey to believe *like* Jesus, we must be clear about the kind of faith Jesus wants us to aspire to. Jesus doesn't want you to simply give your assent to the fact that Jesus believes all things are possible for himself. That would be faith *in* Jesus. Jesus invites you to believe all things are possible for you. That you can do many of the things Jesus does— and even greater things, as written in John 14:12-14:

> *Very truly I tell you, whoever believes in me will do the works I have been doing, and they will do even greater things than these, because I am going to the Father. And I will do whatever you ask in my name, so that the Father may be glorified in the Son. You may ask me for anything in my name, and I will do it.*

125

As you embrace the five beliefs of Jesus discussed in the previous chapters, not just in an intellectual way, but letting them shape your thoughts, fuel your actions, and demonstrate your faith—in other words by having them enter your soul and becoming part of your being—you advance from being a disciple to being an apostle. Like Jesus, you allow God to work through you.

Test Your Water-Walking Faith

Test your water-walking faith by considering each of Jesus' five beliefs and how fully you embody them.

To increase your sense of commitment and vulnerability, I invite you to read each of the following statements out loud:

1. Jesus invites me to believe that there is no separation between me and God, between me and the Holy Spirit, or between me and Jesus. We are full partners, indivisible and united forever.

2. Jesus invites me to believe that my prayers have power. Something happens in the heavens and on earth whenever I pray. The conveyor belt of blessing always moves in my direction.

3. Jesus invites me to believe in a miracle mindset and to make that my superpower.

4. Jesus invites me to have unwavering belief that my life has unique and unreplaceable purpose. I matter.

5. Jesus invites me to believe in the reality of resurrection, to trust that I can rise again by placing more faith in God's future than in fear.

Read these statements more than once as if they are sacred chants. As you read each statement, notice where you stumble, where doubt creeps in, and where your unbelief is revealed. Jesus says, "Everything is possible for one who believes." If, like the father of the possessed boy, you hold a mixture of faith and doubt, ask God to answer your prayer, the prayer of the apostles: "Lord, increase our faith." You can also confess, as the boy's father did: "I do believe; help me overcome my unbelief." If like Peter you are growing in water-walking faith but still give in to doubt when the wind whips or the waves swell, cry out, "Lord, save me." Advancing into apostleship takes more than one leap of faith. It's about constantly refining and up-leveling your faith, noticing and discarding beliefs that limit your faith, renewing the beliefs that build your faith, being willing to let go of doubt and stepping out onto the water—every day.

Just as Jesus needs to know the Twelve are ready to step up their spiritual game, so today, God also wants to know if you are ready to advance from discipleship to apostleship. God is welcoming, inviting, and encouraging you to uplift your consciousness by believing *like* Jesus, and, when you do, to resist evil, injustice, and oppression in whatever forms they present themselves.

You Are a Force to Be Reckoned With

My husband and I love to go to the movies. One of the toughest things for us during the pandemic shutdowns was that the movie theaters were closed. When they finally reopened, we resumed our almost weekly visits to the darkened theaters, accompanied by a tub of popcorn and, for my husband, a large Diet Dr. Pepper.

We find it increasingly hard to find a good movie to watch

together, though, since neither of us is a fan of horror films, and I'm not big on superhero movies either. I've wondered why these two genres have been so popular for the last few decades and even more so now. Maybe it's that, as a society, we are fearful about what's coming next, and we are training ourselves to be suspicious of people and institutions we once trusted. Evil seems to be on the loose, and we want someone to swoop in and fix it.

I have good news and bad news. The bad news is no superheroes are flying off the pages of comic books or movie screens to save us. No superhuman beings with incredible strength, speed, or vision are coming to vanquish the world's evils.

The good news is that it's not nearly as hopeless as superhero and horror movies would have us believe. As a Christian, you come from a long line of miracle workers, healers of the sick, and banishers of demons. Your people proclaimed the gospel of the Kingdom of God since Jesus first walked the earth. So, put away the notion that you have no say in how things go. As an apostle, you are a force to be reckoned with.

We Are the Ones

Jesus lived under conditions similar to yours. Jesus lived in a time of religious and political polarization. Sadducees and Pharisees disagreed on matters of faith, culture, biblical interpretation, and relations with Rome. Neither group saw eye to eye with the Zealots or the Essenes. Each of the four parties related differently to the temple and envisioned different futures for the Jewish people. Independent folks not aligned with any particular Jewish party were often overlooked. Overall, people were upset, torn, and afraid.

In the midst of it all, Jesus stood apart. He didn't align fully with the Sadducees, the Pharisees, the Zealots, or the Essenes.

While he borrowed from the wisdom of each, he kept his own counsel. Instead of following party lines, Jesus preached a vision for the future based on the will of the Father that transcended any single narrative of the day. "Thy kingdom come, thy will be done, on earth as it is heaven." That's why Jesus could have such a diverse following. His "tribe" included a tax collector, Pharisees, independents, Zealots, and temple authorities. Even Romans and non-Jews followed him. And women—many women, who otherwise were much overlooked at the time.

There were trials and tensions with such a diverse following, but one of Jesus' primary beliefs—that he was one with God—lifted Jesus above the fray and activated his agency so he might dare to make a difference and inspire—indeed, send forth—others to make a difference as well. With Jesus at the helm, the apostles couldn't sit around and complain about how bad things were—although they were pretty bad. They had a message to carry. As you learn to believe *like* Jesus, as the Twelve did, you will also activate your agency. You will learn to carry Jesus' message.

Having the faith *of* Jesus will guide you to step into your spiritual power by emboldening you to expand your beliefs from simply believing *in* Jesus to believing *like* Jesus. This vital shift powers your evolution from practicing the faith of a disciple to developing the faith of an apostle. This is a crucial time to look deep within to accept that, as Alice Walker titled her 2006 book of meditations, *We Are the Ones We Have Been Waiting For.*[24] You are one of the spiritual superheroes Jesus is calling on. In this critical time, it's time to look within to acknowledge and accept the spiritual resources deep inside. When you believe *like* Jesus, act with the faith *of* Jesus, and advance from discipleship to apostleship, you not only uplift your spiritual consciousness but you also open yourself to the possibility of having a miraculous impact on those around you. And those far away. You become the change you were always meant to make.

How can you do this? How can you answer Jesus' call to be an apostle, a spiritual superhero, one of the ones we have been waiting for? By completing the challenge of the 40 days to spiritual transformation.

During this season of transformation, you are being unleashed from small-minded beliefs, emboldened by new courage, and strengthened by spiritual transformation so you are free to take actions that make a true difference in the world. This journey calls you to a higher consciousness. Whether it's been four days or forty since you began this spiritual transformation, notice how your world is filled with renewed power and possibility as you release your old beliefs and welcome your new beliefs— the beliefs of Jesus.

Just as Jesus didn't stand still, your spiritual journey is ever upward, ever expansive. Believing *in* Jesus becomes believing *like* Jesus, while faith *in* Jesus dares to become the faith *of* Jesus. Disciples become apostles. Apostles shift the very nature of reality—they become the change they wish to see in the world, and they invite others into this change.

Water-walking faith is exemplified through the 5 A's of Apostleship. Turn the page when you are ready to continue your 40-day journey of spiritual transformation.

CHAPTER 10

The Five A's of Apostleship

Because each of us is gifted with purpose that builds the Kingdom, it's our job to contribute this ray of light to a world threatened by darkness and hopelessness. We need apostles right now. We need a higher consciousness, an elevated way of looking at things.

As we look at the way of the world right now, it's important to remember that the same thinking that got us here is not the thinking that will get us out of here. More of the same won't solve our problems. We need something new. We need a consciousness that embraces the five beliefs of Jesus. In this way, apostles can positively impact the world!

I believe humanity is ready to shift in its relationship with God, to move from thinking of God as an all-powerful but removed being somewhere out there to turning inward to experience their inner divinity. This is the conscious transformation we are ready to make as Christians and as citizens of the world.

Now is the time to take full responsibility for ourselves and our world—to advance from bystander to disciple to bold apostle, from victim to apprentice to agent, by embracing the faith *of* Jesus, by believing *like* Jesus.

In some ways, this is a more natural, organic process than

it seems. Let me tell you a little parable of my own. Call it the Parable of the Caterpillar.

The Parable of the Caterpillar

Do you remember learning the life cycle of the butterfly? The life cycle progresses from butterfly, to egg, to larva (caterpillar), to pupa (chrysalis/cocoon), and then to a new butterfly. I'm not going to focus on the science but rather on the mystery and magic of the transformation. An adult butterfly lays an egg, and the egg hatches into a caterpillar, which eventually transforms into another butterfly. The thing is, the caterpillar doesn't know it's going to become a butterfly. It's a caterpillar trying to live out the best caterpillar life it knows how, eating away at the leaves that help it grow a hundred times its size before it gets the biological signal to build itself a chrysalis (what we call the cocoon), inside of which it will transform itself into the butterfly it was always destined to become. The caterpillar goes through a deep process to become a butterfly, an unconscious process, just as we go through a deep process to become an apostle.

We, too, are destined to transform from caterpillar to butterfly. The difference for us is that our process is a conscious choice. As caterpillar disciples transforming into butterfly apostles, we must choose to intentionally nourish our spiritual practices, give our time and energy to what we believe about ourselves and God, and to adopt Jesus' five transformative beliefs. We must choose to examine our beliefs and conduct these practices until they become second nature, until we take them into our souls, until we emerge from our chrysalis as butterfly apostles with the faith *of* Jesus who can do the same things Jesus does, who can tap into our inner divinity as Jesus does to bring a new consciousness into the world, and with it, new ways of being.

Developing a new consciousness is essential. Believing *like* Jesus reveals your innate power, which emanates from your soul. I believe people who feel empowered from the inside don't have to take power from other people to feel like they are enough or have enough. They don't have to bully or belittle. Nor do they have to shrink to nothing or play invisible to feel they are okay. Rather, people who feel empowered from within are able to bring a new consciousness to all their relationships. Instead of scarcity, there is a sense of abundance. This new consciousness says there is enough to go around—enough love, enough time, enough respect, enough resources—and they are free to give and receive with an open hand and an open heart.

You won't see it until you believe it, but once you believe it, you'll see yourself in Jesus, and you'll see Jesus in you. I believe that your spiritual journey into apostleship is part of Jesus' big dream.

As you practice believing in new ways, with increased faith, together with God, you transform from someone who simply carries these beliefs around in their head as intellectual principles to someone who lives their heart and soul until they become part of your consciousness. And they are transmitted to others in the way you live, love, and lead.

Just as butterflies bring joy, beauty, and hope to others, so does your spiritual transformation from believing in Jesus to believing like Jesus. With this new consciousness, you are a living example of divine unity and partnership with God, the power of prayer, a miracle mindset, a purposeful life, and the reality of resurrection.

The Five A's of Apostleship

Now that you are an apostle, it's time to put your beliefs into action. Use the Five A's of Apostleship as inspiration.

The Five A's of Apostleship are five qualities Jesus accepted for himself and extended to the apostles and thus to you. They inform your mindset, guide your choices, and shape your relationships with God and others in the role of apostle.

1. You are Anointed.

2. You are Appointed.

3. You are Authorized.

4. You are Accountable.

5. You are Ambassadors of the Kingdom.

You Are Anointed

Apostles are anointed. Like the priests, prophets, kings, and deliverers of the Hebrew Bible, who are anointed with the laying on of hands or the use of special oils, you, too, are set apart for a powerful purpose. Originally, in the Hebrew Bible, anointing oil is used for consecrating sacred places, objects, and people for special purposes. For instance, Exodus 30:22-22 notes that the Tent of Meeting, the Ark of the Testimony, as well as the table and all its articles were anointed, as were Aaron and his sons.

In the New Testament, anointing is given by the presence and power of the Holy Spirit, rather than by oil. Anointing means that, guided by the Holy Spirit, you are called, equipped, and protected for a special purpose. God will speak through you to others. As one anointed by God, you will be changed and used. Just as "Everyone was filled with awe at the many wonders and signs performed by the apostles" (Acts 2:43), don't be surprised when you find yourself participating in the creation of wonders and signs, too.

You Are Appointed

Apostles are appointed, as Jesus appointed the Twelve in Mark 3:13-15. They are chosen for a special purpose: "Jesus went up on a mountainside and called to him those he wanted, and they came to him. He appointed twelve that they might be with him and that he might send them out to preach and to have authority to drive out demons." This passage gets to the heart of apostleship: "Jesus ... called to him those he wanted ... that they might be with him and that he might send them out to preach." These are Jesus' messengers and envoys, those he trusts to continue his work.

But being appointed an apostle doesn't end with the original Twelve in the New Testament. After Judas Iscariot hangs himself, the remaining eleven apostles, under the guidance of Jesus, appoint Matthias to be an apostle, bringing the number back to twelve.

Jesus has a plethora of other people he appoints. Jesus goes beyond the Twelve by appointing seventy-two others and sends them out as well (Luke 10:1-11):

> *After this the Lord appointed seventy-two others and sent them two by two ahead of him to every town and place where he was about to go. He told them, "The harvest is plentiful, but the workers are few. Ask the Lord of the harvest, therefore, to send out workers into his harvest field. Go! I am sending you out like lambs among wolves. Do not take a purse or bag or sandals; and do not greet anyone on the road.*

"When you enter a house, first say, 'Peace to this house.' If someone who promotes peace is there, your peace will rest on them; if not, it will return to you. Stay there, eating and drinking whatever they give you, for the worker deserves his wages. Do not move around from house to house.

"When you enter a town and are welcomed, eat what is offered to you. Heal the sick who are there and tell them, 'The kingdom of God has come near to you.' But when you enter a town and are not welcomed, go into its streets and say, Even the dust of your town we wipe from our feet as a warning to you. Yet be sure of this: The kingdom of God has come near.'"

In fact, it isn't just men who are appointed apostles, and it's not always Jesus, the Twelve, or Paul who appoints them. Junia and Andronicus are also known and named as apostles, as found in Romans 16:7: "Greet Andronicus and Junia, my fellow Jews who have been in prison with me. They are outstanding among the apostles, and they were in Christ before I was." Junia and Priscilla (along with her husband, Aquila) are women named as apostles in Romans 16:3-4. Along with several other women, they function as missionaries sent to carry the good news of the Kingdom of God and of Jesus: "Greet Priscilla and Aquila, my co-workers in Christ Jesus. They risked their lives for me. Not only I but all the churches of the Gentiles are grateful to them."

Here's the bottom line: in the Bible, we see a wide range of people who are appointed as apostles: both men and women, both those chosen directly by Jesus and those who never met him in person, both those who served as missionaries and those who didn't; those whose name and stories we know and those who functioned in anonymity.

Do you see that anyone of faith—even you—can be

appointed as an apostle? If you are appointed, if you are chosen, if you feel called by Jesus to be an apostle, Jesus expects you to accept that appointment because, just as more than one Gospel reminds us: "The harvest is plentiful, but the laborers are few" (Matthew 9:37 and Luke 10:2).

You Are Authorized

Apostles are authorized. If you are a church leader, you are, by definition, authorized to be an apostle. It's your call to teach and equip new disciples and apostles for ministry and to call the church towards a Jesus-like dream, even when it gets uncomfortable. But you don't have to be an official church leader to be authorized. Your baptism confers holy authority on you to walk Jesus' path, to believe as Jesus did, and to co-create miracles with God.

And what are you authorized to do? Jesus gives us direction in Mark 6:7-13 (ESV), which offers a slightly different take on Luke 10:1-11 cited above:

> And he called the twelve and began to send them out two by two, and gave them authority over the unclean spirits. He charged them to take nothing for their journey except a staff—no bread, no bag, no money in their belts— but to wear sandals and not put on two tunics. And he said to them, "Whenever you enter a house, stay there until you depart from there. And if any place will not receive you and they will not listen to you, when you leave, shake off the dust that is on your feet as a testimony against them." So they went out and proclaimed that people should repent. And they cast out many demons and anointed with oil many who were sick and healed them.

Jesus authorized the Twelve to work in his name, giving them "authority over the unclean spirits." Today, unclean spirits take many forms—from gossip to judgmentalism, from illness to addiction, and from the degradation of creation to the degradation of people of particular cultures or races. The list is nearly endless.

Here's what is most important: you, as a Christian, are authorized—indeed mandated—to address these personal and societal ills in any way you can. Some of you will work closely with friends and family members who are suffering. Others will feel called to a larger stage. Either way, you are authorized to make a difference. There's a Jewish principle found in the Talmud, "Whoever saves a single life is considered by scripture to have saved the world."[25] Every bit of healing you bring about matters.

Not only that, but God has also given us authority to shape the way the church responds to the world. Jesus summed it up this way: "I will give you the keys of the kingdom of heaven, and whatever you bind on earth shall be bound in heaven, and whatever you loose on earth shall be loosed in heaven" (Matthew 16:19). That means we're not bound by traditions or interpretations of the past. Instead, we are authorized to determine new and appropriate ways to show the love of God to the world around us.

This is not easy work. Even though you're authorized, you'll still face pushback. That's why in Luke 10:19, Jesus says: "I have given you authority to trample on snakes and scorpions and to overcome all the power of the enemy; nothing will harm you." Jesus will spiritually protect you in this important work of overcoming the enemy's power.

You Are Accountable

Apostles are accountable. Jesus believes in people's potential and holds himself accountable for the fulfillment of their potential. This is the drive behind Jesus' healing of so many people. He wants them to be free to live the fullness of their lives. It's also behind his various instructions to the Twelve on the matter of their faith. As we have already seen, Jesus says, "If you have faith like a grain of mustard seed, you will say to this mountain, 'Move from here to there,' and it will move; and nothing will be impossible for you" (Matthew 17:20 ESV). "Everything is possible for one who believes" (Mark 9:23). "If you have faith and don't doubt, you can do things like this and much more" (Matthew 21:21 TLB). These aren't just good ideas for the Twelve to think about. Jesus has taught them, and he knows they can develop this kind of faith. Now they are accountable for living into it.

It isn't just the crowds or the Twelve or the Seventy-Two Jesus believes in. Jesus believes in *you*. Jesus believes *you* can do great things and *you* can co-create miracles with God. As you adopt the Five A's of Apostleship, Jesus calls you to account for developing your abilities. Jesus also wants you, as an apostle, to call others to account to develop their abilities. The Apostle Paul offered this encouragement: "I want us to help each other with the faith we have. Your faith will help me, and my faith will help you" (Romans 1:12 NCV).

What does this faith help us be accountable for? Since we now know that we can move the seemingly immovable—even deeply rooted trees and mountains—we are accountable for bringing light into the darkness, forgiveness and acceptance into our differences, and truth into our chaos. With this accountability, redemption is possible.

You are Ambassadors of the Kingdom

Apostles are ambassadors. Indeed, this is the essential nature of apostleship, as described in the first chapter. Remember, "apostle" comes from the Greek *apostolo*s, meaning envoy, one sent out as a representative or agent. You are one of Jesus' many representatives on earth. In Matthew 10:40, Jesus teaches the disciples what it means to be an ambassador of his: "Anyone who welcomes you welcomes me, and anyone who welcomes me welcomes the one who sent me." Jesus also teaches the Twelve that humility is an important part of being his ambassador. To demonstrate his point, Jesus takes a child into his arms and tells the disciples, "Whoever receives one such child in my name receives me, and whoever receives me, receives not me, but him who sent me" (Mark 9:37). What does he mean? Little children are to be treated as honored and as holy as Jesus. And even Jesus himself is just a vessel for God.

In addition to teaching about humility, Jesus makes a point that allows for all kinds of would-be apostles to be his ambassadors. Soon after Jesus finishes teaching the above parable, John says to him, "Teacher we saw someone casting out demons in your name, and we tried to stop him, because he was not following us" (Mark 9:38). Jesus tells them not to worry about that; they will have inadvertently gained an ally; once that person does miracles in Jesus' name, he'll become a supporter: "For the one who is not against us is for us" (Mark 9:40). There are many ways to be ambassadors of peace and healing for Jesus.

Paul, considered one of the most archetypal apostles of Jesus, accepts and affirms the mandate of apostles as ambassadors as he writes in 2 Corinthians 5:20: "We are therefore Christ's ambassadors, as though God were making his appeal through us." As "Christ's ambassadors," it is our mission to continue to carry out Jesus' mission: "thy [the Father's] will be done on earth as it is in heaven."

Apostleship Transforms You—and the World

By embracing the qualities of the Five A's of Apostleship, you participate in the transformative nature of apostleship. You shift from being a student at the feet of the teacher to becoming a messenger of the teachings yourself.

And what does that do for you? Plenty! You have greater resilience and deeper reserves because you know you are not in it alone. You become proactive rather than reactive. You become energized rather than avoidant. You meet challenges with grit and determination rather than fear and apathy. You are an agent of hope rather than despair. You believe that you can co-create miracles with God just as Jesus did. You are excited by life. You bring contagious energy and enthusiasm into the world. Others feel lighter around you, inspired by your actions and your presence, the grace of God you send out into the world. Your life is transformed. You have become the change you wish to see in the world.

It's an old-fashioned word, "apostleship," with important implications for the present state of the world. Those with agency, authority, and accountability are anointed and appointed to spread the Jesus dream as Jesus' ambassador. Not to support a particular political worldview or institution. Not as disciplinarians for a God of retribution who lords it over us. But as apostles to the Kingdom of God on earth, the kingdom of redemption. To create and support the beloved community. To contribute to a world that works for everyone.

Jesus as an Apostle

There is one more surprise awaiting you in the journey to apostleship. Jesus is an apostle, too! I think of him as the secret apostle. Hebrews 3:1 says, "Therefore, holy brothers and sisters, who share in the heavenly calling, fix your thoughts on Jesus, whom we acknowledge as our apostle and high priest." As an apostle, Jesus himself lives into every one of the qualities of the Five A's of Apostleship.

- **Jesus is Anointed:** Acts 10:37-38 captures the anointing of Jesus in a nutshell. Here, the Apostle Peter is speaking to Cornelius: "You know what has happened throughout Judea, beginning in Galilee after the baptism that John preached—how God anointed Jesus of Nazareth with the Holy Spirit and power, and how he went around doing good and healing all who were under the power of the devil, because God was with him." Not only did God anoint Jesus with the Holy Spirit and power, but the very word "Christ" means "the anointed one."

- **Jesus is Appointed:** In Hebrews 5:5, we see a profound declaration: Jesus is appointed as the Son, while God is the Father. Romans 1:4 reinforces this truth, as Jesus, "who through the Spirit of holiness was appointed the Son of God in power by his resurrection from the dead: Jesus Christ our Lord." The resurrection establishes Jesus' role as the living embodiment of God's promises.

- **Jesus is Authorized:** We need to look no further than John 3:16-17 to see the authority of Jesus: "For God so loved the world that he gave his one and only Son, that whoever believes in him shall not perish but have eternal life. For God did not send his Son into the world to condemn the world, but to save the world through him."

- **Jesus is Accountable:** In John 17:12, Jesus says, "While I was with them, I protected them and kept them safe by that name you gave me. None has been lost except the one doomed to destruction so that Scripture would be fulfilled." In a very real sense, Jesus feels responsible for his disciples and the possibilities they embody. He's protective of them. In John 10:28, he says, "I give them eternal life, and they shall never perish; no one will snatch them out of my hand." His accountability to them is tangible and personal.

- **Jesus is an Ambassador:** Jesus clearly functions as God's ambassador, as he affirms in Luke 10:16: "Whoever listens to you listens to me; whoever rejects you rejects me; but whoever rejects me rejects him who sent me."

In short, Jesus exhibits all of the Five A's of Apostleship. That means apostleship is part of the DNA of faith, of Christianity itself. Just as Jesus is an apostle sent by God, so too are we apostles sent by Jesus.

As the Twelve advance from discipleship to apostleship, something extraordinary happens. They begin to embody Jesus in their own human form in the same way Jesus embodies the divine in his human form. Let me introduce you to a friend who has also begun to embody Jesus in her life through the Five A's of Apostleship.

Living the Five A's of Apostleship: Overcoming White Supremacy in Rural Mississippi

Josie Neill-Browning of Carrollton, Mississippi, found the Five A's of Apostleship indispensable in establishing All God's Children, a community group dedicated to bringing together community members of diverse races and cultures.[26]

Like Alan Layman, whom you met in a previous chapter, Josie also participated in my leadership development program, Creating a Culture of Renewal. This is where she first learned about the Five A's of Apostleship. For her visionary project, which I assign to help the participants put the principles of the Five A's into action, Josie felt called to a ministry of racial reconciliation. She knew it wouldn't be easy to do in Mississippi. "My biggest challenge and my greatest fear were how to accomplish what I felt God was calling me to without alienating most of both the white and Black communities by trying to bring them together." As a layperson in the church, Josie wanted to become a Spirit-led leader, God's co-creator, and help her team members do the same. Josie goes on to explain her vision:

> I believed that if each one of us on the team exercised our God-given abilities our churches would become beacons of light for the area. I thought our two churches could harmonize, capitalizing on the strengths of both in order to help those who were struggling physically, mentally, emotionally, and spiritually in our area. But I realized that wasn't big enough. My vision changed from racial reconciliation to reconciliation of all the divergent cultures and races in our area.

Josie has a vision of UNITY in the CommUNITY. Using All God's Children as the instrument, Josie is endeavoring to co-create with God the miracle of transforming an area once marred by deep racial prejudice, white supremacy, and suspicion of diversity into an open and inclusive community. She envisions a community that is a model of unity amid a nation and world plagued by division and hatred. Here's the miracle she is out to co-create with God and the reality she seeks to one day affirm:

> *Most people in our sister towns will readily accept each*
> *other as equals, despite differences in nationality, race,*
> *religion, culture, class, and wealth. They will seek ways to*
> *interact with each other, to learn from each other, to grow*
> *with each other, and to give all people in the community the*
> *opportunities they need to thrive.*

Why has Josie set out on this difficult path now? Because when everything seemed to be falling apart, the Holy Spirit called out to Josie, "Go! The windows of opportunity are open!" And she felt it was her duty to climb through that window. Even as the world, the nation, the state, and the area she lives in are all divided, Josie strives to heal divisions by starting at the community level. Through All God's Children's programs and activities, Josie and her team bring together people from diverse backgrounds so they can get to know each other as human beings.

Josie believes that God has chosen her team—different people with different leadership styles and personalities—to demonstrate that people of different cultures and backgrounds can get to know each other, love each other, and work together for the good of everyone in the community. Josie puts it this way:

> *I would have never believed that there could be seven*
> *women who would join with me in the quest for unity*
> *and for acceptance of difference. I would never have*
> *believed that we would still be working together three*
> *years after we first gathered. I have seen God, the Holy*
> *Spirit, "I AM," working in and among us, "making all*
> *things new."*
> **Revelation 21:5 (CEB)**

The purpose of All God's Children is not to make everyone all alike but rather to weave together the different and diverse threads in such a way that people respect each other as equals and work together to make every life the best it can be.

All God's Children meetings and programs are open to the community. No membership is required. The group's initiatives have included holiday potlucks, farmers' markets, and classes about the Choctaw Indians who once inhabited the area. According to Josie, these programs have already begun to renew the community in an amazing way. People of different races are coming together and getting to know each other. Out of that, a support group for family members and friends of alcoholics has also formed. Despite the prevailing attitude in this area of Mississippi that "Carrollton will never change," Josie encourages her team to keep their vision before them at all times.

Part of Josie's spiritual journey has been accepting that she can be, and already is, a leader. Out of this work, Josie has personally experienced a spiritual renewal. "I am an anointed, appointed, authorized, and accountable ambassador for Jesus Christ. I am Christ's apostle; I see Him in the work All God's Children is doing in our area."

> Now I am willing to say that I am a leader and to think of myself as a leader, instead of not wanting to claim this role. I didn't want to be a leader because I wanted everyone to like me. And a leader can't please everyone. I am more convinced than ever before that I must heed God's voice speaking to me from the Bible, from devotionals, from inside myself and not get distracted by voices that don't ring true to me, no matter what authority they come from.

Josie, who had always thought of herself as a humble disciple, a follower rather than a leader, is a great example of a disciple called to adopt the beliefs of an apostle—the beliefs of

Jesus. She never expected this calling—she never thought of herself as one who could make a difference—but when the call came, she accepted her new role and the grace of the spiritual transformation that resulted. Her community is the better for it.

If an apostle is a messenger, then every apostle needs a message to carry. Josie's message is diverse groups of people can come together peacefully in community to respect and support each other.

The Five A's of Apostleship solidify what it means to have the faith *of* Jesus. Now it's time to fully and finally throw off the cloak of passive disempowerment.

CONCLUSION

Throw Off the Cloak
of Passive Disempowerment

Churches become sluggish and inward-focused when
they lose a compelling vision of the future. In his seminal
work The Life Cycle of Congregations, George Bullard writes
about this process.[25] As churches age and lose a guiding
vision, management takes the place of inspiration. Structure
takes the place of risk. Stability takes the place of adventure.
And the growth of the congregation first plateaus and then
shrinks. The life of a spiritual community requires constant
renewal to stay true to the call of God. Otherwise, status quo
morphs into decline.

You can say the same about personal spirituality. Personal
spirituality can become sluggish, too: when ritual takes the
place of vision, routine takes the place of risk, and stability
at all costs takes the place of following Jesus. Whenever the
status quo trumps spiritual growth, you need a fresh and vital
spiritual experience to continue to grow.

While Christianity traditionally emphasizes the merits
of discipleship, we must ask ourselves if it is enough to act as
mere disciples or students of Jesus. The truth is that the focus
on discipleship has created a certain amount of passivity. It
seems that Christians are implicitly counseled to wait for
Jesus to "do something" or teach us something—as though

rehearsing his death and resurrection will yield some new insight. Frankly, many Christians—and the churches they are part of—are as hamstrung as national leaders appear to be when it comes to acting with visionary faith on moral and ethical matters.

The 40 days to spiritual transformation is designed to counteract the disempowerment that grips much of our nation, our citizens, our churches, and our church members. Rather than wait on Jesus to impart new teachings, it is time to lean into the teachings he's already given to take the next step in Christian evolution: to advance from discipleship to apostleship by embracing our inner divinity. This spiritual evolution is essential to throw off the cloak of passive disempowerment.

Today, when Christians act as apostles, we enter the world of co-creation. We co-create new partnerships with God, manifest new miracles, pray gutsier prayers, tap into our superpower, unleash the potential of those around us, and courageously step into possibility. It is only by performing these acts with the faith *of* Jesus and by believing *like* Jesus that we can hope to make the world a brighter place just as Jesus did, a world in which all peoples can know themselves to be empowered agents of love, co-creating the very world we wish to live in.

APPENDIX A

A 40-Day Guide to
Spiritual Transformation

In *Believe Like Jesus,* I referred to the biblical idea of
"forty days" as a symbolic period of time—the time necessary
for a fundamental transformation, such as Noah's forty-
day flood to redeem humanity and Jesus' forty-day fast in
preparation for his ministry. Forty days can be more than
symbolic, however. In the Christian calendar, Lent—the time
between Ash Wednesday and Easter—comprises forty days
(minus Sundays, which are technically not part of Lent).
In fact, when I first started writing this book, I thought of
Lent as the perfect time for the spiritual transformation
of the title. The time between Easter and Pentecost is a
similar period of time. As is the period of time between
Thanksgiving and Epiphany. Remember, though, that
spiritual transformation is not a one-time, once-a-year thing.
It is an ongoing process—an ongoing practice—of deepening
belief and spiritual renewal.

I didn't structure *Believe Like Jesus*: *Rising from Faith*
in *Jesus to the Faith* of *Jesus* as a book of daily devotionals,
but I also don't want to leave you without direction for how
to incorporate this spiritual transformation into your life
over the course of forty days. After all, rising from disciple to
apostle is a huge step in anyone's spiritual journey. So here,

I present you with forty brief reflections, one for each of the forty days. Use these reflections as they are or adapt them as a launchpad for your own spiritual practices.

Interpret "reflections" in the way that suits you best. You can read and think about them, take them to prayer, discuss them with a friend or partner, or journal your responses to the questions. You know what works best for you. The important thing is to encounter the themes and ideas of this book in a deeper way and bring them into your own life. As you engage these reflections, rereading the chapters that generated the questions and noting what strikes you as you read would be helpful.

Some of these reflections are adapted from blogs written by Rev. RJ Davis and inspired by my original blogs that led to this book. I use them with RJ Davis's gracious permission.

Toward a More Active Faith

Day 1: For many, the world is a perilous place these days. What keeps you up at night? What do you feel helpless to change? What are you empowered to change? What would energize you to make those changes? Where does faith fit into this prospect for change?

From Disciple to Apostle

Day 2: Spiritual transformation means looking deep within yourself and then acting with the intention to fulfill your God-given potential. List your strengths. Then list the things holding you back. What would it take for you to elevate your spiritual game to co-create miracles with God?

Day 3: What do you think about the distinction between disciple and apostle? Are you a disciple or an apostle? Do you think you can be an apostle? Work the prayer of the apostles into your life throughout the day: "Lord, increase our faith." When you pray this prayer, you join in with apostles around the globe.

Believe *Like* Jesus

Day 4: Your beliefs have power, whether for good or ill. To begin to believe *like* Jesus, you must honestly examine what you currently believe and release those beliefs that no longer serve you. Look closely at the deep-seated beliefs that drive your actions, good and bad. Be honest. In fact, be brutally honest with yourself. Now ask yourself: what would happen if you leaned into God's spiritual power to release beliefs that hold you back?

Day 5: What new beliefs can you consider to further your spiritual growth? How can you use these new beliefs to enact the healing power of faith in your life? How can you shift your consciousness from believing *in* Jesus to believing *like* Jesus?

Believe in Your Divine Partnership

Day 6: Jesus believes that he operates in divine partnership with God. As he puts it: "I and the Father are one." Jesus believes there is no separation between the divine and the human. He further states that "you are in me, and I am in you," meaning his followers are in him, and he is in his followers. By extension, it's the same for us as well. What do you think about that? If you fully accept that God is in you as he is in Jesus, how does that affect the way you walk through the world?

Day 7: Jesus manifests his belief in divine partnership both in words (prayer) and in works (actions). Try this mantra: "You, <your name>, and the Father are one." Say it more than once to draw your awareness from your head, the seat of doubt and fear, to your heart, the locus of your inner divinity. How does that feel? Keep going. Say (or write) a prayer to your divine partner, God.

Day 8: Jesus walked the talk, doing many good works in his time on earth: healing the sick, feeding the poor, teaching others new ways of experiencing God. All of these he did in divine partnership with God. Make a list of the good works you have done—whom you have prayed and cared for, had compassion for, given to, built, or arranged things for. Now celebrate these good works, not for ego fulfillment but as an acknowledgment of God's divine partnership with you.

Day 9: Look for opportunities to partner with God. What can you accomplish if you act on your belief in your divine partnership with all your soul?

Day 10: In stressful times, I imagine my soul enfolding my body. How do you imagine your soul now that you believe you and the Father are one? Really sit with this. Come back to this image in times of doubt and stress.

Believe Your Prayers Have Power

Day 11: Jesus believes his prayers have power. Do you believe your prayers have power? What doubts, fears, bad habits, and limiting beliefs may derail the power of your prayers? What can you do about that?

Day 12: Jesus prays in part as a form of divine communication, a kind of spiritual reflection, to renew his strength and center himself. Create a prayer that asks God to renew your spiritual energy.

Day 13: Jesus also prays for the strength and power of God to work through him, as he does when choosing the Twelve who will carry on his legacy. Create a prayer asking God to work through you to do something big.

Day 14: How do you visualize God answering your prayers? Practice receiving God's answers with an open mind and heart.

Day 15: In Chapter 5, I write, "See everything that happens in your life as an answer to a prayer. Perhaps it is an answer to a prayer you don't even remember praying." This approach is transformative. Everything that happens can be attributed to prayer! Looking back, what in your life has the ring of an answer to a prayer? How can you use this concept to elevate your faith moving forward?

Believe in a Miracle Mindset

Day 16: Jesus' superpower isn't so much performing miracles as believing that he can. He does this by choosing faith over doubt. He has a miracle mindset, a mindset he teaches to his followers. Jesus' miracles are how he shows his oneness with God, their partnership, and the power of his prayers. Do you believe in miracles?

Day 17: Are you a complainer? Complaining is the opposite of the miracle mindset. What do you complain about? Do these complaints deserve your time and energy? What else can you do with the time and energy you spend complaining?

Day 18: Do you have a fixed mindset or a growth mindset? What things, situations, or people do you approach with a fixed mindset? A fixed mindset shuts down your curiosity, your willingness to try new things, and, ultimately, your spiritual growth. On the other hand, what things, situations, or people do you approach with a growth mindset? A growth mindset is curious about how things work, is not afraid to aim higher, and is okay with failing. A growth mindset is a miracle mindset that allows you to co-create miracles with God. What miracles do you see every day?

Day 19: Notice the pattern of your thoughts. Ask yourself: Do my thoughts build my faith? Or do they tear it down? Learn to allow your heart to overrule your head. This is the first step in exercising belief in a miracle mindset.

Day 20: What can you use your miracle mindset for today? What miracles do you want to co-create with God? Ask God what God needs you to do. Then listen. What do you think God needs you to do?

Believe Your Life Has Purpose

Day 21: In the Gospels, Jesus acts on different aspects of his life purpose: Savior, making God's presence widely known, and testifying to God's truth. He lives his life on purpose. Do you have more than one life purpose? What are they? How do these purposes guide both your spiritual life and your life in the world? How can you better live on purpose?

Day 22: If you're unsure what your purpose is, ask yourself these two questions: What makes me come alive? How can I use it to contribute to the benefit of others? The answers don't necessarily have to center on your faith or the church.

Day 23: To better live on purpose, personalize the process by writing out these steps:

List what comes naturally and easily to you and serves a greater good. What are your gifts, skills, and talents? What are your resources? What brings you joy?

1. Note any challenges that arise as you use these gifts to accomplish your purpose.

2. Reflect on how these challenges push you to clarify what you really want and need to do.

3. Now that you've clarified your purpose, what are you able to accomplish?

Day 24: Today, act as if you already live on purpose. What you spend your time on can tell you about your purpose. Write out the itinerary of a typical day. Be specific. Don't just write, for example, "Went to work." Compiling a list of your activities like this can do one of two things—one, by showing you what you spend your time on, the list can guide you toward your purpose; or two, the list can reveal that what you're spending your time on isn't all that worthwhile. What does your list show?

Day 25: Sometimes you already know your life purpose but have trouble accepting it. As your life purpose becomes clearer, list the ways you can live it out. Think of as many possibilities as you can. Say YES to opportunities, requests, and needs consistent with living your life on purpose.

Believe in the Reality of Resurrection

Day 26: To rise from disciple to apostle, we must believe in the reality of resurrection— that new life can come out of dead-end circumstances. Believing in the reality of resurrection throws the window widely open to hope and possibility. Are you a Negative Nelly? What fears are holding you back from embracing possibility? Reframe problems as opportunities and act as such. DARE to dream.

Day 27: DREAM – How can you make a more meaningful contribution to your family, your church, your community, and the world around you? What are your dreams for a more purposeful, faith-inspired life?

Day 28: ALIGN – Who and what can help you make your dream a reality? Spiritual leaders? Mentors? Organizations? Friends? Family? Books, classes, podcasts? Choose influences that elevate you, not drag you down.

Day 29: REALIZE – What are some new and inventive ways you can realize your dream and open yourself to resurrection? Think outside the box. How are the people around you hungry for bravery, hungry for solutions, or hungry for a brighter world? Are you hungry to put your faith into action?

Day 30: EXPAND – The expression of possibility is another form of believing in the reality of resurrection. Forgo perfection. What would you do if you knew you would always rise again?

Water-Walking Faith

Day 31: Do you have water-walking faith, or like Peter, do you falter once you get started? What times in your life have you given in to your doubts and fears? Don't beat yourself up about it. Let it go and aim higher next time by believing *like* Jesus.

Day 32: What times in your life have you overcome your doubts and your fears? Didn't that feel great? Now bottle that feeling, and in other times of doubt, call on the same faith—the faith *of* Jesus—that got you through.

You Are Anointed

Day 33: As a Christian, you are anointed by the Holy Spirit to follow the call to co-creation with Jesus. Are you ready to accept your anointing?

You Are Appointed

Day 34: Not only are you anointed, but you're also appointed. Jesus calls you to be an apostle. You, specifically. How much are you willing to change and grow to accept that call?

You Are Authorized

Day 35: As a friend and follower of Jesus, you have authority to walk Jesus' path, to believe as Jesus did, and to co-create miracles with God. Whether in your personal sphere or on a larger public stage, you already have permission to make a difference in the world. What are some of the ways you can help people in your expanding circles? What are some of the ways you can make a positive impact on the larger world?

You Are Accountable

Day 36: What does accountable mean to you? As an apostle you are accountable to live to your full potential. Jesus calls you to account to develop your abilities, whatever they may be, and use them for to expand love and light in the world. What have you become lazy about? How can you get back into action?

You are an Ambassador of the Kingdom

Day 37: Being an ambassador is the essential nature of an apostle—spreading Jesus' message. Think about Paul and how he carried Jesus' teachings to new cultures and countries. How can you act as Jesus' ambassador? To whom can you carry Jesus' message?

Day 38: As the Twelve advance from discipleship to apostleship, something extraordinary happens. They begin to embody Jesus in their own human form in the same way that

Jesus embodies the divine in his human form. How are you embodying Jesus in your life?

Throw off the Cloak of Passive Disempowerment

Day 39: List and give thanks for the spiritual transformations you have experienced over the last forty days. How has your life changed? How have the lives of those around you changed? Know that this is just the beginning of your life as an apostle.

Embracing the Five Beliefs of Jesus

Day 40: To look back on the spiritual transformation of the previous thirty-nine days and remind yourself what it means to rise from disciple to apostle, read each of the following statements about the five beliefs of Jesus out loud.

1. Jesus invites me to believe that there is no separation between me and God, between me and the Holy Spirit, or between me and Jesus. We are full partners, indivisible and united forever.

2. Jesus invites me to believe that my prayers have power. The conveyor belt of blessing always moves in my direction.

3. Jesus invites me to believe in a miracle mindset and to make that my superpower.

4. Jesus invites me to have unwavering belief that my life has unique and unreplaceable purpose. I matter.

5. Jesus invites me to believe in the reality of resurrection, to trust that I can rise again by placing more faith in God's future than in fear.

Read these statements more than once as if they are sacred chants. As you read each statement, notice where you stumble, where doubt creeps in, and where your unbelief is revealed. Think of ways you can use these stumbles to build on your spiritual transformation from disciple to apostle.

I hope you've found these reflections on the 40 days to transformation helpful on your journey with Jesus. You are elevating your spiritual game—advancing from disciple to apostle by rising from faith in Jesus to the faith of Jesus. Next, consult Appendix B to learn how the "5 Steps to Co-Creating Miracles with God" turns the mundane into the miraculous. These powerful steps will integrate the the five beliefs of Jesus into your daily life.

APPENDIX B

5 Steps to Co-Creating Miracles with God

I am excited to share with you a powerful process for entering the realm of the miraculous! I developed these 5 Steps to Co-Creating Miracles with the help of my leadership team from Creating a Culture of Renewal (CCR). The CCR leaders and I use this process on a regular basis, including when we are preparing for online retreats, when things are hard, and even when things are good. We have shared this process with others in our lives. Even with the spiritual but not religious. It never fails to work.

The 5 Steps to Co-Creating Miracles with God brings about a shift in mindset, allows for the formation of new beliefs, and reveals new actions to be taken. Through this process, marriages have been healed, friendships have been strengthened, family bonds have been fortified, children have been given safe harbor, forgiveness has been offered and received, pastors have been renewed, congregations have been restored, communities have been re-invigorated, visions have been cast, projects have been completed, and new books have been birthed. These personal, congregational, and community miracles have rippled out, touching lives far beyond the miracle-maker, and lapping even onto the shores of eternity.

I believe the questions below are best asked and answered out loud with a trusted friend or colleague. As noted in *Believe Like Jesus,* the scriptures affirm that God created through the spoken word, and that Jesus himself was the Logos, the active word of wisdom of God. While I find this process most helpful as a spoken, declarative process, you may prefer using it as written or meditative reflection.

1. Choose a focus area by asking yourself:

    - In what area of life do I want more miracles or less suffering?

2. Ask yourself one or more of the following:

    - What beliefs and behaviors are sabotaging my natural capacity to allow this miracle?

    - Am I making decisions based in fear rather than faith? What am I afraid of?

    - What would life be like if I trusted in God's positive future instead of my automatic fears?

3. Step into your agency and be sent by Jesus as an apostle:

    - Where is Jesus calling me today?

    - What do I now release in order to be sent by Jesus?

    - What do I now embrace in order to be sent by Jesus?

4. Embrace one of the five beliefs of Jesus and connect with your inner divinity:

   - I believe that God and I are one.

   - I believe in the power of my prayers.

   - I believe in a miracle mindset.

   - I believe that my life has purpose.

   - I believe that resurrection is real.

5. Co-create miracles with God:

   - What miracles am I now co-creating with God?

   - Share this answer with others, joyfully and expectantly.

   - Later, reflect on the miracles made this day as you lived into this process.

Acknowledgments

This book has been a labor of love, contributed to by many. Thank you to the Creating a Culture of Renewal® community for road-testing these ideas on apostleship and contributing to my understanding of what it means to advance from discipleship to apostleship. Special thanks to Rev. RJ Davis for sharing his blogs with me and to the Rev. Dr. Steve Trout for his clarity and delight in discovering more about apostleship and sharing it with me. Thanks to Book in a Barn, and my three other writing groups whose fellow authors provided companionship and accountability. I appreciate early readers, including Beth Allen, Deborah Henson-Conant, Monica Jefferson, Mary Kunce, Bonnie Ives Marden, and Steve Pudinski, who gave me insightful feedback. Grateful thanks to Laura Bush and Charles Grosel of Peacock Proud Press for their miraculous collaboration in bringing these ideas to life. Big thanks to Publisher Kevin Slimp and the team at Market Square Books (especially my editor, Sheri Carder Hood) for believing in me, and for the barbecue. As always, deepest thanks to my husband, Jerry Gonzales, first in apostleship and first in love.

Meet the Author

Rebekah Simon-Peter is passionate about spiritual growth and the communities it fosters. Over the last eighteen years, she has positively impacted thousands of leaders through her award-winning group coaching program, Creating a Culture of Renewal®.

A dynamic speaker and master trainer, as well as a prolific author, Rebekah has engaged and challenged audiences around the country.

Rebekah is a wife, sister, daughter, foster mom, and friend. When she's not hanging out with family, you can find her journaling, hiking on the mountain, at the gym, or enjoying a good cup of coffee.

For more information about Rebekah Simon-Peter, call (307) 333-5990, email office@rebekahsimonpeter.com, or visit www.rebekahsimonpeter.com.

Resources for Renewal

Rebekah and her team offer a wide range of workshops, programs, and coaching services for church leaders and congregations that speed up the process of renewal while reducing resistance to change. For more information on the resources listed below, visit www.rebekahsimonpeter.com.

FREE RESOURCES

- Weekly thought-provoking blogs
- DARE to Dream Like Jesus' plan
- Forging a New Path Study Guide
- Is Your Church Ready for Renewal Assessment

SEMINARS, COURSES and WORKSHOPS

- Seminar: How Christian Ministries are Achieving Success
- Course: Readiness 4 Renewal: Proven Practices to Prepare Your Congregation for Renewal
- Course: Conscious Leadership: Master Your Mindset, Awaken Your Spirituality, and Become an Intentional Visionary

- Workshop: Platinum Rule Leadership for Changing Times
- Workshop: 3 Steps to Engaging Conflict Productively
- Workshop: 5 Steps to Co-Creating Miracles with God
- Workshop: The 3 S's of Post-Pandemic Spirituality
- Jesus-Sized Dreams for Small-Sized Churches

Creating a Culture of Renewal®

Accelerate congregational vitality and interrupt the dynamics of decline by learning to lead with congregational intelligence, leadership smarts, and the ability to shift the culture of your congregation. The results speak for themselves. Churches in our program experience the following miraculous signs of renewal:

- Giving increases up to 33%
- Average worship attendance increases up to 78%
- Missional engagement increases up to 500%

CONFERENCES AND RETREATS

Rebekah speaks at conferences and convocations and conducts specialized retreats for denominational leaders. Visit **www.rebekahsimonpeter.com** to request her to speak at your event.

INDIVIDUAL COACHING:

Rebekah offers individual coaching for leaders who are ready to expand beyond limited thinking and predictable results to transform their personal and professional lives. For more information about these resources and services, visit **www.rebekahsimonpeter.com**.

ENDNOTES

1 Arianne Braithwaite Lehn, "A DNA Test and its Aftermath," review of *Inheritance: A Memoir of Genealogy, Paternity and Love* by Dani Shapiro, The Christian Century, June 5, 2019, p. 38.

2 Abraham Lincoln, *Lincoln: Speeches and Writings: 1859-1865*, Library of America; annotated ed., October 1, 1989.

3 *Dictionary of Biblical Imagery*, Leland Ryken, James C. Wilhoit, and Tremper Longman III, eds., IVP Academic; first ed., November 2, 1998.

4 The biblical passages in this book are cited from the New International Version (NIV) revised in 2011 unless otherwise noted.

5 Rebekah Simon-Peter, *Dream Like Jesus: Deepen Your Faith and Bring the Impossible to Life*, Market Square Publishing, 2016.

6 https://www.ucg.org/bible-study-tools/booklets/you-can-have-living-faith/our-faith-in-christ-or-his-faith-within-us, accessed June 11, 2024.

7 https://www.ncbi.nlm.nih.gov/pmc/articles/PMC3667744/, accessed April 17, 2024.

8 Larisa Heiphetz, Elizabeth S. Spelke, Paul L. Harris, and Mahzarin R. Banaji, "The Development of Reasoning about Beliefs: Fact, Preference, and Ideology," https://www.ncbi.nlm.nih.gov/pmc/articles/PMC6438088/, accessed June 11, 2024.

9 Bruce Lipton, *The Biology of Belief: Unleashing the Power of Consciousness, Matter & Miracles*, Hay House, 2016.

10 Thomas Merton, *The Contemplative Life: Its Meaning and Necessity.* Reprinted in *Thomas Merton Early Essays 1947-1952*, edited by Patrick F. O'Connell, Liturgical Press, 2015.

11 Ethan Zell, Amy Beth Warriner, and Dolores Albarracín, https://www.ncbi.nlm.nih.gov/pmc/articles/PMC3678767/ Accessed September 28, 2024.

12 https://en.wikiquote.org/wiki/Pierre_Teilhard_de_Chardin, accessed April 25, 2024.

13 Simon-Peter, *Dream Like Jesus*.

14 https://journals.sagepub.com/doi/10.1177/0031512519888304, accessed April 25, 2024.

15 https://www.ncbi.nlm.nih.gov/pmc/articles/PMC10387721/, accessed April 25, 2024.

16 Nina Lesowitz and Mary Beth Sammons, *What Would You Do If You Knew You Could Not Fail?: How to Transform Fear into Courage*, Viva Editions, December 17, 2013.

17 This counting of miracles only includes specific miracles. It does not include general miracle stories like the passage from Matthew 15:29-31. These general miracle stories occur throughout the Gospels.

18 The word synoptic comes from the Greek and means "seen with one eye." The term synoptic points to the similarity of the accounts found in the Gospels of Matthew, Mark, and Luke. It's thought that all three gospels draw from one source document. The Gospel of John, however, is thought to have come from a different source document which helps explains why many of the stories, and even vocabulary, found in this gospel are so different.

19 Rebekah Simon-Peter, *Forging a New Path: Moving the Church Forward in a Post-Pandemic World*, Market Square Books, 2022.

20 Carol S. Dweck, *Mindset: The New Psychology of Success*, Ballantine Books, 2007.

21 https://bustedhalo.com/ministry-resources/lessons-from-st-teresa-how-to-be-the-eyes-hands-and-feet-of-christ, accessed June 11, 2024.

22 Wayne Dyer, *You'll See It When You Believe It: The Way to Your Personal Transformation*, William Morrow Paperbacks, 2001.

23 Gil Bailie, *Violence Unveiled: Humanity at the Crossroads*, PublishDrive, 1996.

24 Alice Walker, *We Are the Ones We Have Been Waiting For: Inner Light in a Time of Darkness*, The New Press, 2006.

25 https://rac.org/blog/save-one-life-save-entire-world-including-yourself, accessed June 5, 2024.

26 Much of the following is summarized or excerpted from Josie Neill-Browning's project paper, "How I Created a Culture of Renewal," submitted to Rebekah Simon-Peter's leadership program, Creating a Culture of Renewal.

Other Books by Rebekah Simon-Peter

Green Church
Reduce, Reuse, Recycle, Rejoice!

Green Church Leader Guide
(with Pamela Dilmore)

7 Simple Steps to Green Your Church

The Jew Named Jesus
Discover the Man and His Message

Dream Like Jesus
Deepen Your Faith and Bring the Impossible to Life

Forging a New Path
Moving the Church Forward in a Post-Pandemic World

Made in the USA
Las Vegas, NV
05 March 2025

19065282R10105